T0145933

the power of

NET

magic

the power of
NET
magic

HOW TO **RAISE** YOUR **ENERGY** LEVELS
&
ATTRACT LOVE INTO YOUR LIFE

SUSAN BARNES

Advantage™

Copyright © 2006 by Susan Barnes

All rights reserved. No part of this book may be used or reproduced in any manner whatsoever without prior written consent of the author, except as provided by the United States of America copyright law.

Published by Advantage, Charleston, South Carolina.
Member of Advantage Media Group.

ADVANTAGE is a registered trademark and the
Advantage colophon is a trademark of Advantage Media Group, Inc.

Printed in the United States of America

ISBN: 978-1-59932-014-4

Most Advantage Media Group titles are available at special quantity discounts for bulk purchases for sales promotions, premiums, fundraising, and educational use. Special versions or book excerpts can also be created to fit specific needs.

For more information, please write: Special Markets, Advantage Media Group, P.O. Box 272, Charleston, SC 29402 or call 1.866.775.1696.

Dedication

This book is dedicated to

Dr. Jim Bischoff,

an amazing human being.

Acknowledgements

Special thanks are in order for the following people:

Dr. Richard Bandler

Hope Van Vleet

Ann McIndoo

James Bonnet

Joan Rhine

Edward Bryant

And a special thanks to Natalie Lang for the outstanding job.

She typed this manuscript for me.

TABLE OF CONTENTS

INTRODUCTION

The idea for this book was birthed in Brisbane, Australia, in the springtime. My friend Nicki Vee and I walked through the halls of the Royal Pines Resort when a man I've never met smiled as we walked past him.

When Nicki asked me if I knew him, I replied I didn't and joked that he must be in "my net". She looked at me and said, "What do you mean?" It was then that the idea bubbled up inside me and I wondered to myself, "What if we all have nets?" What if we all have invisible nets of energy that flow in and out of us continuously, creating a magnetic pull that people can't resist or a net of energy that repels people away from us?

What causes this? You've met people you love being around. You don't know why, you just do. And you've also met people who being near were the equivalent of hearing fingernails on a chalkboard. You couldn't get away from them fast enough. I thought of all the times when people were responsive to me and the times they were indifferent. What was the difference? And how could I create that moment again when they were the most receptive? The other question that came up was that if I could teach myself how to do this, could it be taught to others?

Like a dog with a bone, I couldn't let this go. After experimenting, I came up with a visualization called **The Net**, which has since evolved into **The Power of Net Magic**. This technique has been expanded and has proven effective for people in attracting love partners, husbands, wives, babies, wealth, friends and, more recently, health.

There is so much we are capable of creating for ourselves and others including immense bliss, joy, pleasure, and happiness, but we stay stuck in ineffective patterns. Others can see this, but we can't seem to find our way out of it.

Life is a whole lot easier than we think, and it's a whole lot more juicy fun than we have been having. Let's get on with the fun stuff. Let's find the person we want to be with and let's go into the business we want to be in. Ready?

Let's live the abundant life we are meant to live.

Come on. Take my hand. Let's walk, skip, or run into your new life. Take a deep breath. That's right, close your eyes and with a smile on your face: **DIVE IN!**

chapter one

THE **FOUR LEVELS** OF THE **NEW CONSCIOUSNESS**

"Real spirituality is realizing that when you vibrate real joy, the people around you will begin to do the same."
-Richard Bandler

- The Consciousness of Happiness
- The Consciousness of Unconditional Love
- The Consciousness of Freedom
- The Consciousness of Perception

THE CONSCIOUSNESS OF HAPPINESS

The consciousness of happiness is to be happy now, no matter what. I have a friend who is always laughing and smiling. When I hear her voice or get an email from her, I feel good all over. Happy people create an environment you are drawn to. Happiness is beauty. To be happy is to go into an altered state of consciousness that transcends all levels of being.

My friend is a potter who lives in the mountains of Colorado. She's a bit overweight, wears no makeup and is missing a front tooth. She once told me that her husband accidentally threw away her false tooth. She started to giggle and I giggled, too, until we both laughed so hard we could barely breathe. When we paused long enough to take a breath she said, "I'm glad my husband married me for fun."

I think about that statement often and I realize that beauty and love come from joy, and joy radiates from the soul like the sun.

For too many years I allowed myself to go into a negative and depressed state of mind on a consistent basis. It became such an addiction that even during funny moments I'd catch myself laughing and then remember I was depressed and I'd go back into a negative state. How ludicrous is that?

Have you ever noticed what kind of people and situations you attract into your life when you're in a negative state? You attract negative and depressed people. Like attracts like. It's an irrefutable law. What we think about, we become. And what we think about permeates the atmosphere all around us. Think happy thoughts and you'll attract happy people. Try doing something really fun.

I like to see how long it takes to bring another person out of a negative state. It usually takes just a few seconds because all that's needed is a smile to change someone's state, even your own.

Negative thought patterns are an addiction, just like drugs or alcohol. And like substance abuse, negative thinking abuses your mind, emotions, physical health, and your spirit. Desire positive thoughts and happiness. Desire joy more than you've ever wanted anything. Become happy and watch the new kind of people and experiences that come into your life.

Say to yourself: "I am happy. "I am completely and totally happy." Or, "I radiate joy, love and peace wherever I go."

Keep saying those phrases throughout the day and watch as you begin to see the world differently. Watch how people respond differently to you. Even people who are already in your life will change as you do. If there is someone you know who seems to bring out the worst in you, start to think of that person in a positive light.

I once had a friend who I was very close to. We were as close as sisters for many years. Our children were the same age and played together on a regular basis. We had a disagreement and both of us allowed our egos to get in the way, each of us justifying why one was right and the other one was wrong.

This went on for almost six years until I began to think of her in a positive light. Suddenly the disagreement seemed ridiculous. I thought of all the fun times we had buying toys for our kids and going in search of the perfect tostada all over town.

I thought of her in a positive, loving light. One morning about a week after I changed my thoughts about my friend, my daughter Chantal and I drove downtown. When we parked, another car drove up and parked next to us. As I glanced over, I saw my friend. We smiled, got out of our cars, and hugged each other. It was if we'd never been upset with one another. When you change your thoughts about a person, miracles will happen.

journal page

Date_____

Write down someone you know who about whom you have had negative thoughts. Write about them as if you and this person were in perfect harmony. Write about how you <u>want</u> to see or feel about them. Do not write about what you <u>don't want</u> to happen. Whatever you focus on will come into your life. When you focus on what you want you will draw it to you. Likewise, when you focus on what you don't want you will draw that into your life.

THE CONSCIOUSNESS OF UNCONDITIONAL LOVE

When my son Alex was born, I had great difficulty during the birth and my heart stopped briefly during the process. During this experience, I will never forget how I felt when I saw an angel so massive he literally covered the ceiling. As his arms lifted me up, I felt a feeling of bliss so powerful that I had never known even existed before that moment.

Time moved like thick water and when I looked back I saw the people in the operating room moving as if they were in a fast motion. I heard their thoughts, felt the fear in the room, and could actually see the surgeon's brain ticking off all the steps to save my life and Alex's. When I turned back around, I was in a place like a large bright tunnel, all the while feeling totally blissful. I remember I felt a voice. I didn't hear it but felt it, and the voice told me I could go with them or I could go back. The first thought that came up was my children being without a mother. I knew they still needed me in their lives.

I went back into my body – slammed back is a better description. Even though I was in a perilous situation, my only thought had been of my children, not of myself.

Unconditional love is loving with no expectations, no demands, and with none of the lower energy forms of jealousy, possessiveness, addiction, neediness or code-pendence. When you love yourself unconditionally, you can begin to love others. When this happens, you attract miracles into your life because your energy is irresistible to all things that vibrate at similar levels.

journal page

List ways in which you can become even more irresistible.

THE CONSCIOUSNESS OF FREEDOM

Freedom is in the mind. It's a state of being; it doesn't exist in the physical. To experience freedom, one must first know what it's like to not be free.

Freedom is an illusion just like time is an illusion. Time is what we know and must create to have a sense of order in our lives. Order is the foundation that we need to experience so we can begin to step forward into being aware of our own mastery.

Some of us choose a lot of order that lasts throughout many lifetimes and some of us choose to create order in a short amount of time and once mastered, let go of. If someone lives in disorder, you can rest assured that their inner and outer life is in disarray as well.

Once while watching the Suze Orman discuss finances on her television show, I heard her speak to a woman who called in with a question about finances and new relationships. Suze asked the woman if the man she was involved with had a lot of clutter around his yard and in his house. The woman hesitated then answered yes.

"Then he has debt, "Suze answered. "And do you really want to start a life with someone who has debt?"

After thinking about this, I realized Ms. Orman had a point. Looking back on people I've known in my life, the ones who lived in cluttered surroundings did have the lack of money as one of their issues.

There are exceptions to the rule, but most of the time this is the case. Where there is clutter there is disorder. And more often than not, the person who lives in a messy environment also lacks harmony in the spiritual emotional, mental, and physical levels. When disharmony is present, very often it will show up in their financial state.

I had a friend who would often say that he appeared in my life to teach me about freedom. Now I hadn't asked this person to teach me about freedom because to me he lived his life as someone in emotional bondage. This man had constant money challenges. He had never been responsible emotionally or financially for anyone except himself and he was dishonest with himself and with me.

The first step to freedom is through truth. I had to face the truth about this person.

When you decide to become completely honest with who you are and with everything that you have created in your life, then you can begin to be honest with others. Being honest with others is the next step toward freedom – honesty being defined as having no exaggerations and not withholding the truth.

A man I had been in a relationship with told me that he hadn't told me about his unfaithfulness because I hadn't asked. That's a form of dishonesty. There was a time in my life when I, too, was dishonest.

What we give out comes back to us. It doesn't matter whether it's energy, a physical action, a lie or the truth, it will return from where it was created.

Freedom occurs when we've known responsibility. It can't happen otherwise. Freedom also occurs with truth; there is perfect order in truth. To know freedom, you first must experience its polar opposite and come to terms with that. There is a fine line between freedom and imprisonment, which is its polar opposite. Just like selfishness and selflessness. When you experience true selflessness, whether it is through raising children; taking care of a sick person; working for another; living through giving and being selfless with joy; or not being a martyr, but a fully loving, giving, happy person; then you move into true freedom.

Love with no expectations.
Be honest.
Be free.

In the words of Richard Bandler, "Freedom is everything and love is all the rest."

journal page

Date_____

What has to happen in order for you to feel free?

THE CONSCIOUSNESS OF PERCEPTION

According to Cicero, "A happy life begins with tranquility of mind." One of the most important elements in reaching different levels of consciousness is in our perceptions. Two separate people can experience the exact same thing and yet afterward, they will both have a completely different account of what occurred.

I used to attach expectations to outcomes. I needed to have an outcome for every event that happened to me. Did this color my perception of people and events before I even experienced them? You bet it did! I gave the term *control freak* a whole new meaning.

When you expect a certain outcome for every single interaction in your life, you are attached to the illusion that you are not only controlling the event but that you have control of the other people involved in the interaction.

All of us begin life with the question, "Who am I?" Our unconscious minds ask this question over and over, and it carries over into our conscious lives. Any time a question is asked, our unconscious mind searches for an answer and brings it to our conscious awareness through our thoughts and actions. Along with that basic question of "Who am I," we also ask other questions that affect the kind of people and situations we attract into our lives.

The question I used to ask myself was, "What's the end game?" Because of this question, I became attached to the outcome of any situation, whether it pertained to business or to personal relationships. "What's the end game" is the same premise as "What's in it for me?"

As a result of my old question, the word game brought out a competitive energy in me and this created a competitive dynamic between me and anyone I became involved with. When you're constantly concerned with what you can get out of a relationship then what you get is simply more lack, or less love.

In the past I felt I had to "win" all the time. I always looked for and created an "end" to every situation, going so far as to sabotage relationships because I had to control the beginning and the end. It's in realizing that there is no "end" that one starts to see that every interaction is simply an exchange of energy, and what kind of energy you put out is what you get back.

If I'm unconsciously thinking what is in it for me, I will attract a person with the same motivation. So then you have two people with an agenda – an agenda to get the most they can out of what they perceive the other person will give to them. Where's the truth in a relationship like this? It's virtually non-existent.

As a result from this type of thinking, I suffered from many aliments including depression, insomnia, stomach aches, and always feeling like I was not achieving enough.

False beliefs create sickness. And when someone believes they must control an outcome, they are living in dishonesty. They are selling out their spirit to the highest bidder. Because we are so finely tuned, every single cell in our bodies down to our DNA is completely affected by our thoughts. If my thoughts are not of the highest intention, I have released negative energy into my body and that negative energy acts as a toxin.

When I perceive that the person I'm interacting with is their higher self, they will (at some level) perceive this about themselves. And when I perceive that I am my higher self at every moment, my interactions will be completely different than they were when I operated under my old question of what was in it for my benefit.

My new question is:

How can I create with the highest intention in order to heal others and myself?

Do you think this changed my interactions with people? It did immediately.

journal page

Date_____

1. List all the things and people who make you happy, and then list what you can do to become happier.

2. Write down what unconditional love means to you. How can you begin to love yourself unconditionally? When you are finished with this writing exercise, go to a mirror and look at yourself with love. Tell yourself you love every part of you.

journal page

3. What does personal freedom mean to you? What actions can you take today to become free? Is there someone you need to forgive and let go of? Is there a project you want to start?

journal page

Date_____

4. Today when you wake up, perceive that everyone you meet loves you. How does this feel?

5. What question can you ask yourself that would change your level of awareness? Questions such as: How can I serve? How can I be taught to love even more? Think of an empowering question to ask yourself.

chapter two

HOW TO LOVE YOURSELF UNCONDITIONALLY

Until you love yourself, you won't be able to love others. As I sat in a coffee shop writing this chapter, a beautiful baby looked up at me and smiled. I smiled back and she and I laughed. We had so much fun having complete rapport with one another. The thing I noticed most about the baby was her complete joy of being alive and in the moment. This smiling, happy baby loved herself and everything else in her world.

We all start out like this. We're happy babies, glowing with love for ourselves and everyone in our environment. Then something happens – we hear our parents argue, we aren't matured, we encounter bullies, or perhaps a caretaker doesn't take care of us.

We receive negative programming through parents, grandparents, siblings, relatives, teachers, kids, or entertainment. And before we know it, we've amassed a myriad of doubts and disabling beliefs. We may even accept the idea that we aren't worthy of love, so we stop loving ourselves.
I'm convinced that on an unconscious level we teach what we need to learn.

I had a challenge with loving myself unconditionally. After attending seminar after seminar, going to therapy, listening to self-help programs and reading over a thousand books on personal growth, I reached the point where I stopped listening to others and about how they learned to love themselves. I finally realized

I had to come up with a plan that worked for me and came straight from my heart. I knew I had to look at every relationship I'd ever had in my life including my relationship with my grandparents, my parents, my brothers, and my sister. From there I went to every friendship I'd ever experienced, going as far back as I could remember all the way up to the present. Then I brought up all the romantic relationships I've ever been in, no matter how brief, no matter how painful. I went over every single one. I wrote down how we met, the first thing I remember thinking about the person, how it turned into a relationship, and the ending from my point of view.

When I finished with all of the listings and had written down all the feelings, thoughts, and emotions tied to each relationship, I went back and wrote about every relationship from the other person's perspective. Even though I didn't know for a fact how the other person experienced being in a relationship with me from their perspective, I tried to imagine how they felt. (When you do this for yourself, you'll notice how certain patterns show up in every relationship regardless who the relationship was with.)

I realized that I had tended to be a pleaser to the degree that I gave my power away in every relationship, whether it was in a friendship or a romantic situation. This became such a pattern for me that I noticed I tended to get into relationships with people I didn't really want to be with. I created the programming that I was not worthy of love. This belief stemmed from the core thought that I did not love myself unconditionally. When you don't love yourself unconditionally, blissful relationships are always out of reach. So, I could never find a happy, satisfying relationship because I did not love myself yet.

One of the key distinctions I made was that I had to make it a must to let go of what others thought or felt about me. The more I loved myself, the easier relationships became because I taught myself how to become less and less dependent upon others' moods, words, feelings, and thoughts about me. When I accepted myself, I began to accept others at an entirely different level. My relationships shifted to deep, soul-stirring experiences.

The other notable thing that occurred is that I started to attract a different type of person into my life like people who lived at higher standards. A giant shift occurred in my life and I liked it.

In the following exercise you are asked a series of questions about your family. If you did not have grandparents or parents, or siblings, create imaginary ones or choose people in your life who were like a family member such as a teacher or mentor.

exercise for loving yourself unconditionally

Write down your thoughts to the following questions the space provided. Answer each and every question. If an answer doesn't seem to come easily write the following: What do I need to know about my experience with this person? Then go on to the next question, and when you're ready go back to that question and answer it.

Your unconscious mind will bring the answer to you.

1a. What is my first memory of my grandmother?

1b. What is the best memory of my grandmother?

1c. What lesson did I learn from being her grandchild?

1d. I am grateful to my grandmother because:

1e. What would you say to her if she were in the room with you now?

2a. What is my first memory of my grandfather?

2b. What is the best memory of my grandfather?

2c. What lesson did I learn from being his grandchild?

2d. I am grateful to my grandfather because:

2e. What would you say to him if he were in the room with you now?

3a. What is my first memory of my mother?

3b. What is the best memory of my mother?

3c. What lesson did I learn from being her child?

3d. I am grateful to my mother because:

3e. What would you say to her if she were in the room with you now? Remember, anything you say is perfect. You can scream at her or you can speak lovingly. The key is to go with the first thing that comes up.

4a. What is my first memory of my father?

4b. What is the best memory of my father?

4c. What lesson did I learn from being his child?

4d. I am grateful to my father because:

4e. What would you say to him if he were in the room with you now?

5a. What is my first memory of the first time I fell in love?

5b. What lesson did I learn from this experience?

Continue to answer the questions for the following people who have been in your life:

- Romantic partners
- Teachers who played a pivotal role in your life
- Friends
- Pets
- Children

chapter three

THE **SEVEN** **ENERGY CENTERS**

Sanscrit Name	English	Spine Location	Organ
Muladhara	Root or Sacral	Fourth Sacral Vertebra	Gonads
Svadhishthana	Spleen	First Lumbar	Spleen, Pancreas, Liver
Manipura	Solar Plexus	Eighth Thoracic	Adrenals
Anahata	Heart	First Thoracic	Thymus
Bishuddha	Brow	First Cervical	Pituitary Gland
Sahasrara	Crown	None	Pineal

When we begin work on the chakras it is important to start from the lowest chakra and to work your way up the body. This symbolizes the evolvement into spiritual mastery, much like the way we move up through the grades in school until we finish. To have a constant flow of energy into the river of complete awareness, the energy systems (or chakras depending on what you prefer to call them) must be open and in vibrant health. You can check each chakra to maintain their balance through meditation.

The detection of any health issues created by a blocked chakra will become apparent with your growing awareness. You will become aware of a blockage within your body, and you'll know intuitively how to clear it with ease. Restoration of flow will occur as you rise to a higher vibration, attracting into your life love that resonates at a higher frequency.

Know that you are divine. Be certain of your divinity. Life is eternal; your soul is constant. The way you live your life is being birthed by you in every single moment. You create the kind of life you choose with every thought. Thoughts form simultaneously with pictures and pictures coincide with words.

Words create feelings. Feelings ebb and flow in a continuous motion. Do you base your decisions on feelings? Do you feel propelled to make a decision to avoid a negative feeling? Or do you move forward to feel a positive feeling?

What's showing up in your life now? How is your money situation? Are in lack or abundance?

What is your love life like now? Are you in a happy, emotionally, and physically rewarding relationship? How do you feel when you are with your partner? Do you feel good or bad? Do you feel complete or incomplete?

Think about your friendships. Pull up in your mind each and every one. Go over each one. How do you feel with each person? What does your heart say? Does the friendship bring out the best in you? Yes or no? How does each friend feel to you? How do you feel around them? Empowered or not?

Are you ready to open the curtains and let in the light?

The way to let in the light is to clear out any blockages in the energy systems in the body. According to most meditative philosophies we have what are called chakras throughout the body.

The chakras or energy centers are so powerful when they are awakened that you can literally manifest what you want when you want it when they are working for you, not against you. When they are blocked, they can repel what you want and need for your evolution. When they are clear, they make your life blissful.

The way to creating the life you desire is to move up and beyond your current level of vibration. In order to change your vibrations, you must first change your thoughts.
What is your life like now? Is the life you create, sometimes consciously, most of the time unconsciously? Your unconscious thoughts give birth to conscious thoughts, creating the patterns you follow and the strategies you have developed.

Can you imagine a passionate, joyous, blissful life dripping with so much abundance and love that you change the lives of others just by existing? That's right. Imagine it now. A warm golden light pulsates around your body. Feel it as it pours in and out of you, and with every breath you take your light gets bigger and brighter.

Hear the rushing sound of the light as it washes through every cell in your body coursing through your veins and feel yourself growing stronger with the energy going in and out. Watch the light pour out of you like tidewater and see it as it covers a wide territory.

You are a sun, the boldest light in the universe. When you walk by, all living beings flourish and see the beauty of their souls. You are a spreader of love, joy, happiness, growth and abundance. An infinite source of wisdom is within you and every moment in time brings you closer and closer to conscious awareness.

> As you step though each door
> of consciousness you will find
> yourself suddenly aware.
>
> Open your hand, here's the key.
> Are you ready to discover the
> secret of awareness?
> Read on ...

HOW TO CLEAR YOUR ENERGY

Let's dissolve all unpleasant karmic issues now. That's right. Put your hand in mine. It's time to move forward; it's time to move on.

People often ask me these questions: "How does karma affect my present relationships?" and "How can I avoid a bad karmic relationship with someone", or, "Is it possible to avoid karma with another person or situation?"

Do we create karma (good or bad) with others? Yes. Do we create agreements with others before we come into this life to fulfill a karmic debt? Yes. Must we suffer in order to work out karma with another person? No.

If we have made an agreement with another person, that must be acknowledged. Acknowledgement means recognizing the divine in the other person and accepting their essence where each of your levels of evolvement is at the moment of reuniting with each other. Your souls have agreed to the "repayment" of any debt before both of you were even born.

You will be placed into a position of being able to give them what they need at the right time. When it has been given, and you will know this in your heart, it is time to <u>let go</u> and <u>move on</u>.

Don't become a jailer of grudges or ill will. To do so forces you to become a prisoner also, and the cycle continues, accruing more and more unpleasant karma as time goes by. The instant you let go, the bad karma ends. You are free.

Freedom is the first step toward your evolvement. Freedom first, love will follow.

When the concept of letting go is fully understood, experienced, and surrendered to, the process of attracting love at the soul level begins.

Soul mate has been a term used without full awareness of what the term actually means. A soul mate is someone with whom your spirit is perfectly attuned at the instant of creation. Many lifetimes slip by where soul mates may meet but not be together in the physical sense because each has other aspects to work on that need to be brought out by different people.

There are soul ties you may have with others that you may be joined with as mates, lovers, or co-workers. Do not confuse this with soul mate. A person you have a soul tie with is not the same as a soul mate.

To prepare yourself to attract love into your life, you must first clear your energy systems otherwise known as chakras. The following list reviews the chakras in your body.

- The Root or Sacral chakra
- The Spleen chakra
- The Solar Plexus chakra
- The Heart chakra
- The Throat chakra
- The Brow chakra
- The Crown chakra

The root chakra which is also known as kundalini is the catalyst for physical energy. It's used for instinctual, unconscious functioning and is the source for life-producing energy. The root chakra propels us into taking action. It controls the entire gonadic system. This chakra vibrates to the colors of pulsating red/orange.

Next is the spleen chakra which regulates the endocrine glands. This chakra also controls the pancreas and the liver. This chakra will often have a blockage in people who are alcoholics. The spleen chakra vibrates to the color rose pink. It is an activator as well as a transmitter of energy.
When the root chakra is blocked, the spleen chakra goes into hyper-drive by expelling energy that is already in motion. This is what's commonly called the experience of a "second wind." When this occurs it gives the root chakra a chance to kick start itself.

Rich, lush green is the color representing the solar plexus chakra. This energy is life preserving and sustaining.
The job of the solar plexus chakra is to allow exactly the perfect amount of energy to the adrenal gland so that the correct amount of adrenalin is in our bodies.

When the root chakra is blocked or over stimulated the person will become overly emotional and ruled by the emotions by feeling upset or angry. This over stimulation of the root chakra will cause the solar plexus chakra to be unable to handle all the excess energy. When this occurs, a number of ailments can result from stomach aches, ulcers, irritable bowel syndrome to other stomach diseases.

If the root and the solar plexus chakra stay in conflict with each other you have two very powerful energy systems working against each other. The result can be devastating and end in creating cancer or other life-threatening diseases.

Some external causes for the root and solar plexus chakras to become out of balance are the following:

- Caffeine
- Sugar
- Unbalanced diet
- Pornography
- Sexual addiction
- Sex with an agenda, or where there is no love.

The Heart chakra is next. Its color is shimmering gold. This is where energy is transmitted into pure energy. The immune system depends on the clarity of the heart chakra, which governs the entire immune system.

All of the energies of the lower chakras are held by the solar plexus chakra and pour into the heart chakra, becoming golden rays of powerful energy. In the physical and the spiritual, the heart chakra is the purifier, the transmitter, and the translator.

The lower energies must be sorted out and fused together in the heart chakra or they can't flow fully into the higher chakras. This is the place where the higher and the lower energies come together.

The next chakra, the throat chakra, is where the ego can control. The thyroid gland is represented here. A deep electric blue is the color or this chakra. The throat chakra represents our willpower. This is where any kind of power struggle is manifested. This is where you see highly spiritual people or people with great knowledge get into trouble.

The ego is a powerful thing and unless it is acknowledged and tamed it can take over our lives. On the flip side, we need to learn how to harness the energy of the ego so we don't fall into becoming a "victim."

When the egos of each person, the student and the teacher are out of balance, a victim/controller energy occurs where the student slips in the victim energy and the teacher goes into controller energy. The relationship then becomes codependent, causing both people to stay stuck at one level of consciousness.

The easiest way to step into a new level of consciousness is to change who you hang out with. If you have difficulty moving on from a particular teacher, you are "hooked". It has become a codependent relationship.

When a victim stops being a victim, the energy transforms from the energy of force to the energy of unlimited flow.

When a controller stops controlling other people, the energy shifts from restraint to expansion.

People in abusive relationships can fall into this category too. Their throat chakras become blocked when they are unwilling or unable to express themselves.

Any energies coming from the heart chakra must be fully expressed in the throat chakra. Freedom of expression and creativity reside within the throat chakra. This energy system governs the thyroid gland. When someone isn't fulfilling their creative needs they may suffer from thyroid challenges. If a person has no restraint in expressing themselves and hurts people with careless words or indulges in gossip they very often suffer from hyperthyroidism. On the other hand, a person who doesn't speak up when they should will suffer from an under-active thyroid.

The best way to keep the throat chakra clear is simply speak the truth. Not to the degree where you hurt another person, but with tact and honor. Truth is the best gift you can give another person and the best gift you can give to yourself.

In the words of Gary King, lecturer on *The Power of Truth*, "You were not put on this Earth to protect another's feelings, you were put on this Earth to speak your truth. Lying is the cause of dis-ease." King goes on to challenge people to only speak the truth for twenty-four hours with no exaggerations and no embellishments – just the pure and simple truth. Try the 24-hour truth challenge yourself, and you'll notice an immediate shift in your energy patterns.

The next chakra is the brow chakra. This chakra is connected to the functioning of the pituitary gland and the nervous system. This chakra is responsible for breaking up energy, refracting it, and sending it throughout the body via the other chakras. This is the chakra where the balance of acid production and alkaline production is maintained. When balance has been achieved, it is no longer necessary to waste any extra energy. The brow chakra vibrates to the color indigo, which is a mixture of primary colors. It's important to note that each color of every chakra has a specific tone when cleared out. When the chakras are clear, the tones within are in perfect harmony throughout the body.

When the brow chakra is in harmony with itself and the other energy systems in the body then you will experience "enlightenment."

Next is the crown chakra. This chakra is represented by the color purple. It is where the third eye resides. When the seventh chakra is fully activated, there is no longer the need for ego. Total enlightenment occurs and an avatar is created. Purple turns into the white fine light of purity where all bad karma is burned away, resulting in the complete light of love.

As you learn how to create a constant energy flow throughout the energy centers in your body, you will begin attracting higher vibrations into your life. When the energy centers or chakras are stagnated, depending at which level, we attract into our lives people with equal blocks. As the saying goes "Like attracts like." My grandfather used to say "Water seeks its own level."

We clear our energy systems through awareness, meditation, truth, and by honoring one another. By integrating all of the energies into one, there is complete harmony. After all, we are all connected to one another. We are divine. We are creation.

When you have a thought, it becomes a living thing. What the thought does once it's formed depends greatly on what kind of thought it is!

When energy flows freely through the cleared chakras, you instantaneously evolve. As you are evolving, you attract into your life a mate at an equal or higher state of evolvement.

Stop now and notice your pattern of breath. Do you breathe high up in the chest? From your belly? Are your breaths deep and constant, or short and shallow?

visualization for energy clearing

Begin to slow your breathing. Take in deep breaths, and as you do, visualize that every breath you take is filled with healing energy that flows into your body and bathes all of your organs, restores your blood to perfect flow, and fills your being with healing light.

Now imagine that with every breath you breathe, this healing, shimmering breath of life is cleansing all the chakras inside you. These breaths pour in love and light, and bring peace into your chakras. Each of these breaths dissolves any and all past barriers from your energy systems.
Picture in your mind the old blocks dissolving the way soap bubbles dissolve away dirt. See the old residue fading away and being replaced with pure, delicious loving energy. Feel bliss.

Throughout the rest of this chapter, pay attention to your breathing. Continue cleansing, dissolving the blockages and feeling the peace.

When you have gone through every chakra and cleansed each one with your healing breaths, imagine that with every breath you take, you are with absolute certainty healed of any blockages in your energy system. And with every breath you exhale, imagine that any blocks you may have had are simply gone. Listen to the sound created by your chakras. Close your eyes and listen. What do you hear?

Watch as the blocks quickly release. One right after the other. One, two, three ... gone, like dominoes falling one right after another ...four, five, six ... discover how easily they go because they no longer exist.

The energy of love now flows though you with your chakras functioning as a tunnel for this phenomena.

Your spirit and mind are integrated with your emotions and your body so all are working together in complete harmony.

When our body, heart, mind and soul work together, there is a rhythm that occurs and beats in conjunction with the rhythm of the Earth. When you tap into this ancient cadence, you will take a massive leap into your conscious evolvement. To evolve, one must be conscious. To be conscious, you must be fully aware. To be fully aware, you have to **WAKE UP**.

When we are conscious, we become aware of who and what we attract into our lives. When someone enters your life, be aware of the kind of energy that person sends out.

What words do they use, what is their language pattern, negative or positive? Is their presence uplifting or not? How do you feel around that person?

If you feel agitated or believe something isn't quite right, even though the outward signs seem fine, then listen to your intuition.

Is there a reason we meet people who enter our lives? Yes.

Do we have to become involved with every person we meet? No.

One way to avoid bad karma with another person is to acknowledge that person, hold them in a light of love and honor, and move on.

Do you want to get out of a negative relationship or one that is nonproductive? You want to know when your karma with this person is fulfilled? It is fulfilled when you let them go. Give yourself permission to release them.

If you are in a destructive relationship, bless the other person out of your life. Do it now without looking back. You will not meet the right love for you, for your life, until your energy field and your chakras are clear.

If you are currently in a relationship that is stagnant or nonproductive and you stay there all the while hoping another person will enter your life to take you out of the situation, then you are fooling yourself.

If we are in a dire situation, the instant we become aware that we must survive and we let go of whatever self-imposed prison we have gotten ourselves into, help will arrive – help we create with the unconscious decision that the life we lead is not acceptable.

Have fun with life!

According to Richard Bandler, the creative genius behind Neuro-Linguistic Pro-gramming, "When I started Neuro Hypnotic Re-patterning I decided that people were not having enough fun. It's not that you are not capable of it, it's just that you are not using your neurology that way. I want to get people out of the personal jails that they build for themselves and then you'll have greater freedom because all my work is about <u>personal freedom</u>."

Personal freedom. Two words to live by. When we are free of our self-doubts, our self-imposed limitations and out molded beliefs, *we become free.*

If love is what you search for, the secret is to start by being free.

Freedom precedes love.

Give yourself the freedom to be your higher beautiful self. When we are free, others find us irresistible.

Throughout the meditations and visualizations in this book you will learn how to clear your energy systems and coast into a new, uncharted realm of consciousness.

You begin evolving at a faster rate and attracting people and circumstances that are also at a higher vibrational state of being. The key is to take action and do the meditations described. Act upon the knowledge. Don't just sit back and read at a passively conscious level. When you participate in the knowledge imparted in this book, your life will change dramatically for the better.

journal page

Date: _____

List where you think you have been blocked and why. Are you ready to clear out all of your energy systems? How will you look, sound, and feel when your chakras are clear?

chapter four

CHANTING
INTO CLARITY

Chanting is as old as time. To find your body's natural rhythm, chant until you actually become the chant. Look at the following facts about sound:

- Sound is an integral part of the clearing process.
- We all vibrate sound.
- Certain types of tones can either strengthen or weaken the body.
- Language resonates to tonality.
- Words heal.
- Music heals.
- Chanting is the key to the secret of life.

Breathe in deeply. Exhale. Breathe in exhale and say "Om."

Breathe in deeply through your nose. Exhale and say "Om."

- Breathe in through your mouth. Exhale through your mouth saying "Om."

The word Om is an ancient power source for diving into the deepest levels or awareness.

- Say "Om" in a whisper four times. Every time you utter the word Om know that your energy centers are opening and vibrating.

- Say "Om" louder for four times. Allow the word to resonate through out your body, spreading strength like a lotus flower within your spleen chakra.

- Now begin to chant "Om" in a strong, deep voice. Fill your energetic field with this new clear energy. Feel bliss spread within your body.

- Say "Om" loudly and clearly. Picture the word as a bubble and see this bubble grow bigger each time you say Om. Surround yourself with the powerful supernatural protection of the word Om.

Breathe in through your mouth and breathe out.

Say Om with a smile on your face and in your heart.

journal page

Date: _____

How do certain sounds affect your mood? List any sound or music that makes you feel uplifted, and a few sounds where you have felt agitated. What can you do to listen to more of the sounds you like? How does chanting affect you?

chapter five

THE **AWARENESS** OF **LOVE**

Your subconscious mind is the gateway to unlimited possibilities and often holds the answers to any challenges you may have faced in your life. The reasons for all challenges are stored within your unconscious mind as are the solutions to these challenges. For every problem you encounter, there are multiple solutions created simultaneously. Einstein said, "The solution to the problem you create will be found at a different level of consciousness than the problem."

Your unconscious mind will be your guide in attracting the love you want. But first you must leave behind your past love strategies and go to a new level of consciousness to formulate a new strategy.

Have you ever experienced a sudden insight or an intuition about a situation or a person and that intuition proved to be correct? That's an example of your subconscious and your conscious mind becoming aware. When you train your brain to become aware of your strategy for making decisions at the unconscious level, you will experiences flashes of intuition. This will no longer be sporadic occurrences, but as a constant state of being.

Can you see that for every challenge you create, the answer is born? There is no problem created that a solution isn't available as well. Anything else would be impossible. In physics the law is that for every action there is an equal and opposite reaction. Also, in life for every thought there is an acknowledgement of that thought by the universe.

There is constant communication occurring between all things in this world and in other dimensions – constant reactions. Have you ever had the experience of feeling as if you were being watched, and you turned around to see that someone was staring at you? Energy follows attention.

When someone thinks of you, or you are thinking of them, does the phone ring? Or you suddenly receive an email and it happens to be from that very same person? Cool, huh? We are always transmitting our thoughts, feelings, and emotions. Others pick up these transmissions on a subconscious level.

Who you are speaks louder than words. Who you are enters a room before you do because your thoughts and the answers to any and every challenge you have created for yourself lies within you. The reason you have created the challenges you experience on a physical, emotional, or spiritual level is a part of your evolution based upon what your soul has chosen.

For every challenge created, there are multiple solutions birthed simultaneously. They will continue to pop up until you recognize them and bring them to life by solving the challenge.

(NOTE: For simplicity's sake, in this book I speak on what has been my experience and learning which as occurred through the conscious, subconscious mind, and the superconscious mind. I also refer to the subconscious as the unconscious mind.)

In *Conversations with God*, Neale Donald Walsh says, "The first step in changing anything is to know and accept that you have chosen it to be what it is. If you can't accept this on a personal level, agree to it through your understanding that we are all one. Seek then to create change not because a thing is wrong, but because it no longer makes an accurate statement of who you are."

If you want to change anything in your life, realize first you're where you are because of a decision you made either on a conscious level or a subconscious one. The key is to be present in every thought and action so that you can begin to bridge the gap between your superconscious mind, your subconscious, and your conscious mind. Your subconscious holds the answers to any challenges you have in your life.

James Bonnet says in his book *Stealing Fire from the Gods*: "The conscious and the unconscious minds work very closely together. Information passes easily between the two worlds. The unconscious mind is omnipresent. It knows all and sees all that is happening within and around the conscious mind. The unconscious mind communicates with the consciousness by means of insights, feelings, premonitions, mental images, intuitions, dreams and so on ... The conscious mind can communicate with the unconscious mind as well. We do this when we use our creative imaginations, when we ask ourselves questions, say our prayers, meditate, create fantasies, or dream. When we dream, the conscious mind ventures into the strange and fantastic world of the unconscious."

Your unconscious mind will be your guide for attracting the love you want. First you must leave behind your past love strategies and go to a new level of consciousness to formulate a powerful strategy.

Have you ever experienced a sudden insight or an intuition about a situation or a person and that intuition proved to be correct? My friend Brenda is highly intuitive. when we want to get in touch with each other I will simply think about her and she'll call within five minutes. It works the other way around, too. She'll think about me and I'll email or call her within five minutes of receiving the thought.

When these types of things happen – an intuition, sudden insight a dream that comes true – these are all examples of your subconscious and your conscious mind working together to bring you into awareness.

If you want to approach someone to talk to them or ask them out for coffee but you've convinced yourself that this person isn't going to be interested, change the way you think about them. See them in your mind as being receptive to you. Play it out in your mind. See yourself approach them with confidence. See the other person simile at you. Hear yourself speak to them and imagine the other person saying yes to your invitation. Feel positive about the interaction.

I used to be very shy and would rarely speak to anyone unless they spoke to me first. This caused me a lot of pain because I wanted to be around people but held back. When I really thought about it I realized it was because in my mind I assumed I wouldn't be liked. I would actually picture the other person's face looking at me as if they didn't like me.

One time I watched a woman who met people with ease. Even if she wasn't greeted wholeheartedly, this didn't stop her. She would continue to greet complete strangers and smile and they would smile back as if they were long-time friends. After getting up the nerve to approach her, I asked her how she made friends so easily.

She smiled at me and replied, "Every morning when I wake up and every night before I go to bed, I say to myself, everybody loves me and I love myself."

That statement marked a shift within me that allowed me to look at my interactions with others in a different light. I say the same statement to myself and I've added something to it. This is what I say every night before going to bed and when I wake up in the morning and throughout the day: "Everybody loves me and I love myself."

After saying those words, they settle into my unconscious and become a belief. Shyness is no longer an option.

There is continuous communication happening between all beings in this world and in other dimensions. Constant action, instant reaction. We are always transmitting our thoughts, feelings, and emotions. Others pick up our transmissions on a subconscious level.

Your thoughts and patterns create a rich field of energy that surrounds you and others pick up on this energy field. Have you ever met someone you just like being near? You can't really explain why, you just like hanging out with that person.

When you choose to be happy, no matter what, then love appears. Think of all the times you've been happy. When you laughed and couldn't stop. How do you feel in those moments? You feel love, love for being in the moment. When you're happy, you're radiating love and this is the most powerful, irresistible attraction of all.

steps to take to become aware of love

1. Make a list of all your past love relationships.
2. Write down everything that happened in the relationship. What were the challenges?
3. Who ended the relationship? How and why?
4. What is the common thread in all of your relationships?
5. Can you remember a time when you felt completely loved?
6. Write down all the times you felt completely loved.
7. Write down next to each of these times exactly what happened. Who were you with? What did they say if anything and what did you say to them? What was their tone of voice? Did they speak fast, slow or in between?
8. Now write if it was bright or dark? Is this memory close to you or far away? When you felt loved during these times, where is the feeling location in your body? Point to it right now.
9. List all the things that make you feel loved. For me it's the following: (Use these or make up your own.)

a. Sunny day
b. Walking
c. Petting an animal
d. Seeing a baby
e. Giving
f. Learning

Sometimes we have too many rules in place in order for us to feel loved.

Take the list you wrote for questions 1 through 8, smile, crumple up the paper, say thanks... and throw it away!

Start another list and think of all the simple things in live that can make you feel loved.

1.
2.
3.
4.
5.
6.
7.
8.
9.
10.

The simpler you make it, your awareness for all the love you're capable of experiencing will far surpass anything you've ever dreamed of.

exercise - dissolve unrewarding love strategies

I taught this fun little trick to myself when I was a child. I call it melting. When I feel confused or find myself going into a negative state, I see a different world and anything I want can be in this world and anybody can act the way I want them to. This is how you do it:

> Make your mind go blank. Now see in the center of your mind a window looking out into space.

> See yourself sitting in a chair in the middle of a room.

> Look out the window, see the stars and the planets. Find a planet you feel drawn to.

> Make the planet come closed to the window. Now literally melt and travel out the window into the planet.

> Become you again as you are now recently.

> What does your planet look like?

(In mine there is a lush jungle, the colors are penetrating, deep greens and bright oranges. The flowers are big and the sky is a beautiful rich sunrise in vibrant colors of pinks, purples, and smoky grays. The scents are the scents of the flowers so rich and delicious that I am a part of the yummy smells.)

> For a moment, turn and look behind you. See yourself as you used to be when you chose unrewarding love patterns.
>
> Now make that picture dim. Make it dark and gray and see it melt.
>
> Turn now to the present in your beautiful new world and see yourself create a new, rewarding love strategy.
>
> You now attract beautiful, blissful, joyous love strategies. If one doesn't work, it melts into the rich ground and another forms and grows its place.
>
> Like a flower, pick this new rewarding love strategy. Close your eyes and breathe it in until it becomes a part of you.
>
> Reward yourself with the gift of love.

journal page

Date: _____

Please answer the following questions:

What challenges am I facing in my life right now?

What thoughts have I thought before and during this challenge?

journal page

Date: _____

If I were in a room, sitting at a round table with seven people of my choosing, living or dead, to help me with this challenge, who would they be?

What would each person advise me to do in order to solve this challenge?

chapter six

HOW TO **CHANNEL** THE **ENERGY** OF YOUR CONSCIOUS AWARENESS INTO YOUR UNCONSCIOUS MIND

How do you enter the energy fields you need to make the connection between the conscious and the unconscious mind? Focus on directing your asleep (unconscious awareness) into your awake (conscious awareness) and visualize that energy as a stream of light that shoots out from one to the other.

We all emit an energy field around us. There are people with great wealth and they always attract money into their lives or opportunities to make money. These people are in the energy field of wealth. Likewise, there are people who will attract love and great relationships into their life. They are in the energy field of love. And the same can be said for people in poverty. They are in an energy field of scarcity.

How do you enter into the energy field that you want to be in? Read on...

visualization for entering the fields of energy

See in your mind the energy field of complete, unconditional love. What does it look like to you? What sounds do you hear? How does it feel?

When you have the energy field of love in your mind, see it as a spinning vortex of whirling colors in shades of rose pinks, hot pinks, and shimmering violet. Notice the gradients of layers and look upon the center of this energy field.

There is a space of complete calm that surrounds this spinning vortex. Hear its silence.

On the count of four you will step into the space surrounding the vortex of love energy.

1. Breathe deeply, exhale and blow out into space.
2. Breathe deeply through your nose, exhale and blow into the space.
3. Breathe deeply through your mouth and exhale saying "Om" in a low tone.
4. Breathe in deeply through your mouth and exhale saying "Om" in a lower tone.
5. Now take a deep breath, hold the breath, close your eyes and step into the space of silence, exhaling as you do so saying "Om."

Be silent. Experience the sensation. Float in this space and allow yourself to be pulled toward the swirling mass of energy inside the vortex.

As you float through the silent space, you will suddenly notice a door appear, see it opening, revealing the most intense colors of pink, fuchsia and lavender you've ever seen.

Float through the door and feel yourself moving forward into the energy field of love.

Spin as fast as a whirlpool, experiencing every level of love cascading from a rushing current to a slow moving stream of energy until you suddenly find yourself in the direct center of the eye of the vortex. Feel the power of exhilaration and the rush of bliss as you are the very essence of pure, total, complete love.

What do you see? What do you hear? What do you feel?

You now are always within the energy field of love as it is within you. You vibrate at the highest level of love. This begins the process of attracting the love you want into your life; this is a process that once started cannot be stopped. Love attracts love.

journal page

Date: _____

What will help me step into the energy field of my choosing, whether it be love, abundance, health, or spirit? What is the one action I can take that when I do it, I will know I'm in the energy field?

List the action and a reason for choosing this action if you are aware of it.

chapter seven

WHAT KIND OF LOVE DO YOU WANT IN YOUR LIFE?

How do you decide what kind of love you want in your life? The first thing is to go for what you want, not for what you don't want. Many times when I ask people what kind of person they want, they always tell me what they don't want.

When you preface a sentence with the word *don't*, you may in fact get that very thing because the unconscious mind doesn't process the word don't. Have you ever noticed when you say to a child, "Don't touch that," the child goes right up and touches whatever it was you wanted her not to touch?

Adults are the same way. The ego is like a child and will do whatever it wants and it will rebel against you because it wants to be in control at all times.

I used to say, "I don't want a person with low energy in my life." And guess what I attracted? Exactly what I didn't want!

We give power to what we don't want when we focus all of our energy on that particular thing.

Figure out what you want. When you decide what you want, your unconscious mind will go to work and will help you in attracting the people you want in your life.

exercise for attracting the right relationships

Go to a quite place. Lie down and close your eyes. Ask yourself the following questions:

- What kind of love do I want?
- What kind of person do I want in my life?
- What are his or her values?
- What kind of standards do they have?
- What do they do?
- What is their mission in life?
- How are they in a love relationship?
- Are they honest?
- What do I want?
- What do they look like? Does it matter?

Breathe in and hold to the count of ten with the questions above in your conscious awareness.

Open your eyes and write down exactly the kind of person you want, including their likes and dislikes.

Write as much as you want. Write in as much detail as you can think of. When you are finished writing, read what you have written out loud. Now picture in your mind's eye the person you have written about.

See all the qualities you want this person to have: compassion, honesty, playfulness, the ability to communicate at a deep level, the ability to love fully and unconditionally, someone with the same type of work as you, their mission.

Look at this person. See you and this person meeting and looking into each other's eyes. Embrace each other.

Hear the other person's voice. What do they sound like? How do you sound when you speak?

What feelings are flowing through you as your are in their presence and they in yours?

Now freeze this picture and imagine the image is on the cover of a playing card. Take the card, breathe in deeply, blow out into the card, and fill the image with energy. Place the card into the palm of your hand blow it away, releasing the card into the universe.

Know with absolute certainty that the love want is here now for you.

chapter eight

HOW TO CHANGE DYSFUNCTIONAL PATTERNS

The first thing that must be done before dysfunctional patterns can be changed is that you must recognize the pattern you are in.

A friend of mine named Kathy had the pattern of dating emotionally abusive men. Did men who were loving and caring come into her energy field? Yes, but her radar wasn't picking up on them. Her sights were set for abusive men. She had to change her way of thinking before she could stop dating this type of man.

It can run the range from men or women with substance abuse problems, married people, or people already in relationships but who are unfaithful. The first step in changing anything is to know what it is.

I recently listened to Dr. Phil show on the radio while I was driving. The subject was mothers-in-law and future mothers-in-law. A woman was going to be a mother-in-law was creating disharmony between her son and her son's fiancée because of her behavior.

It became abundantly clear to the audience and to me that this woman was blatantly crossing boundaries. But when Dr. Phil asked her why she thought her son and his fiancée were saying the negative things about her, she answered that she didn't know. Her voice made it clear that she had no conscious awareness of the behavior she produced that caused such dissention.

The mother-in-law was dropped in unannounced any time she felt like it. The daughter-in-law came home one day to find that her mother-in-law was in the house showing it to her friends without even asking permission.

Dr. Phil told the woman repeatedly that nobody (not even him) likes it when guests drop in unannounced.

We have certain behaviors or patterns that were cultivated since childhood, scripts that we created to protect us in some way, but are no longer serving our adult selves.

Recognize the patterns you set up. If, for example, you have a pattern of attracting emotionally unavailable lovers into your life, then start by looking at what you are doing to pinpoint how you are running this strategy. Once that is done, unleash it and come up with a strategy that serves you!

I had an issue with friendships. Because I stayed so busy with writing, teaching, coaching, running a business, and raising three children, I literally had no time left for friendships.

One night I had a dream where I was sitting on a small step and in front of me was a large wooden door with imposing black ironwork across it. I tried to open the door and found it to be locked. When I looked down, I saw a bunch of large keys. I tried to open the door with every single key and none of them worked.

After what seemed like a long time, I gave up and walked away. I climbed up a hill and looked back. To my surprise, I saw a massive field with a door in the middle. It had only been a door. All I had to do was to simply step back and I would have seen it for what it was.

Sometimes we become so focused on something and we get ourselves stuck in a pattern of trying key after key to find the solution when the solution is something entirely different! We have to step away, or step forward, or step sideways to find the solution. And when you go in a different direction, let go of all emotion tied to the problem at the same moment you change direction.

I have a successful real estate business and have always been able to come up with the best strategy for making money in this business. When asked how I did it, the first thing that came to me is I have never had any emotions tied to the deal.

Lose the emotion and allow reason from your unconscious mind to give you the answers you search for.

As I said, friendships have been a challenge for me, but looking back I can see the reason for the problems. I allowed people into my life who had an agenda. Rather than my choosing to be friends with them, I had allowed other people to come into my energy field who had no business being there.

It wasn't until I went to see Richard Bandler speak that I became aware of the tendency of choosing a dysfunctional pattern for relationships. During class, Richard pointed out that he wanted me to choose other people I wanted to be with. He taught me how to keep away people I wasn't interested in and draw in people I am interested in.

Richard said to me, "Use your energy to pick up when someone is going to come over to you and with that energy, stop them so they don't have to come across the room to approach you when you aren't interested...If there is someone you want to come over to you, use your energy to draw that person to you."

I tried to figure out what he meant and how to use my energy to block someone I didn't want near me so I came up with the following plan.

I see colors around people and have since I was a child, so I decided to use this gift. When I walk into a room where there are a lot of people, there are so many different colors around that it can be overwhelming, so I use the dimming technique where I dim the colors.

Now, after learning from Richard Bandler, I go into a room and begin to dim it gradually. This allows the people with the most interesting colors around them to stand out. When I see someone with colors that I am attracted to, I simply imagine a pathway open up and I see their color or their auric field gravitate toward me.

If someone with colors in their auric field is someone I am not interested in, or if I see or feel they are about to come to me, I use a golden color to shoot out from my aura and form a wall until they move on.

This technique can be used in other areas such as business opportunities or wherever you want. When it's done this way, the person you aren't interested in saves face and moves on to someone who is interested. Everybody's happy! Isn't that what it's all about?

Bliss is the ultimate goal.

My tendency in the past was I didn't stop to look at what a person's standards were or even whether we shared similar values.

I was recently friends with a woman I will call Roxy. She kept insisting on our becoming friends. Even though my gut instinct picked up that something wasn't quite right, I became friends with her anyway. It soon became apparent to me that she and I had very little in common and also that she could be quite manipulating. Her favorite pastime was spending thousands of dollars on Seventeenth century costumes and having tea parties. This was important to her, but not to me.

She invited me to every tea party which required that I would have to fly to the West Coast in order to attend. She became increasingly angry each time I politely refused. During every phone conversation we had, she let me know that if someone made her angry she dumped that person and never spoke to them again. I remembered asking her if she at least alerted the person that they were about to get the heave ho and she replied, "They know what they have done."

Now, was that a red flag? You bet! A red flag the size of Texas, but I still hung in there. Oh, I shouldn't omit that this woman had also informed me she was a diagnosed schizophrenic on psychotropic medication. But, I am an open-minded person and so I stayed in the friendship.

Well, as you can imagine, my time as this woman's friend soon came to a close. I called her, she didn't answer, nor did she return my calls. A friendship ended. Now, should I have been surprised at all? No, she told me who she was from the beginning. She was a person who ended friendships on a whim. She told me this many times. People will tell you who they are. All you have to do is listen. I chose not to at the time.

As I thought about this friendship, I saw all the signs. We had virtually nothing in common. She was broke most of the time and depended on her grandmother to bail her out of debt. I even gave her money a few times to she could get by. When she had money, she blew it.

On the other hand, I have always been a saver and if my bank account goes to a certain amount, silent alarms go off in my head and I work to regain the money. I've never depended on relatives to bail me out of a bind. I figure I got there myself and it's my responsibility to get myself out. Plus I welcome a challenge and love to figure out solutions to challenges. Just one of our many differences, but...

One of the easiest ways to change a dysfunctional pattern is through sustained action. The keys are:

1. Recognize the pattern.
2. Use sustained action to change a pattern.
3. Find an action to take.
4. Know your outcome.
5. Create an action-based script.
6. Do visualization for friendships.
7. Take action right now.

I reached a saturation point with the friendships I had. No longer would I tolerate or get into a friendship that was dysfunctional. I wanted to change it immediately! Here's what I did:

1. I recognized the pattern.
2. I changed my language. I started saying to myself, "I attract loving friends and prosperity."

Always remember that the universe is constantly manifesting for you what energy you put out. The universe wants you to be completely happy, wealthy, and in loving relationships. It searches for ways to give you those things.

In the Bible it says, "Ask and you shall receive." All you have to do is know what you want, ask for it, and believe that you have it.

And the other key is to ask for exactly what you want, not what you don't want.

Remember that the unconscious mind doesn't process the word *don't*. If you say "I *don't* want a mate who lies" or "I don't want a friend who is a user," guess what? You will draw into your life precisely those very people.

I took action by outcome planning and doing the friendship visualization. I wrote my friendship script. I knew what I wanted in my life and the kind of people I did not want in my life. I also raised my standards. When you raise your standards, you raise your level of consciousness. When your level of conscious awareness is raised, you attract people of a higher awareness like you.

The following is a story of love written by Richard Bach:

> There is a colony of creatures living under rocks at the bottom of a raging river. One day, one of these creatures decided to stop clinging onto the rocks. He released himself, surrendering to the flow of the current. At first, the creature tumbled about and smashed into the rocks and weeds of the river.
> But, instead of returning to a clinging life, he continued his journey. Soon he learned the way of the river and his trip became fast and enlightening.
> Weeks later, he passed another group of creatures clinging to the rocks in the same way that he had before. One of the creatures saw him coming and screamed to his peers, "Behold the messiah has arrived."

journal page

Date: _____

Do I choose the people in my life or do they choose me? List the reasons and if you want to change your behavior.

When now would be a great time to change a relationship that no longer serves your highest purpose and vision?

chapter nine

TO **LOVE**
IS TO **LET GO**

As a child I went on family vacations during the summer to Pike's Peak, Colorado. My parents stayed in a 100-year-old cabin called the Preacher's cabin because a preacher built it and lived in it.

Isn't curiosity great? When my parents went off trout fishing, I was left to do whatever I wanted – play hide and seek with the chipmunks, pick flowers, whatever...One time I decided to go exploring in the forest. To me a forest was a safe place because there is only honesty there. There are no words in the woods.

After I walked quite a ways through the trees, I came upon a small hill covered in luscious green grass and exquisite flowers.

When I got to the hill, I sat down and leaned against a tree. I suddenly realized I was lost and went back into my mind to retrace my steps. As I went over my past steps, I saw the most beautiful creature I'd ever seen in my life.

My grandfather used to tell me stories all the time about this creature, a silver badger. "A rare and ferocious thing," my grandfather said. As I watched this "rare and ferocious thing," sniffing the grass and moving toward me, I became mesmerized by its beauty while simultaneously I knew that a silver badger could and would kill me. I became a part of the tree by letting go of all thoughts and being a tree.

The badger walked past me as if I weren't there.

When I knew he was gone, I stood and retraced my steps back to the Preacher's cabin where the chipmunks waited to play again. In order to let go of fear, you must do so at the unconscious level. When you try to let go consciously you set up a battle with the ego. As soon as you focus on the thought, "I don't want to be afraid," guess what you're going to attract? Yep, fear.

When I became focused on something other than myself(the tree), I became curious about the nature of the tree and the fear vanished because I was no longer focused on it.

Nature has no comprehension of a vacuum. If a vacuum occurs, nature refills it. When your life is cluttered with chaos, with sticky situations, and challenges you have created such as toxic people, then there is no room energetically to attract the love you desire into your life.

All things have an energy pattern. There are people with a low vibrational energy and people with a high vibrational energy. And one can go back and forth between low to high, and back to low again.

Symptoms of People with Low Energy Patterns

- They say they will do something, yet they won't follow through.
- They have little or no integrity.
- They are dishonest.
- They go to work but give as little effort as possible to their employer.
- They complain about their situation yet do nothing to change it.
- They blame their lack of finances on everyone except themselves.
- They get caught up in pretty details.
- They file lawsuits.
- They hang onto relationships that are dysfunctional because of fear.
- They are fear-based.
- They are addicted to substances.
- They won't take care of their bodies.
- They degrade themselves by allowing people to use them.
- They blame others.
- They won't take responsibility after committing a crime.

- They take advantage of others who are in an inebriated or unconscious state.
- They are unconcerned about the environment.
- They are unconcerned about animal life.
- They are apathetic.

The list could go on, but you get the point.

One time I complained to a friend of mine that I felt I had been taken advantage of financially by someone who I trusted. "I was used," I said angrily.

"Someone can't use you without your permission," was his answer.

And the more I thought about what he said, the more it dawned on me how acutely accurate that statement was. I did open the door to allow that person to use me. After that lesson, I now no longer give people such permission.

People you want to attract into your life will now have a high vibrational frequency.

In order to attract these people you must raise your vibrational levels. The quickest way to raise your vibrations is to do these things starting now:

1. Meditate or pray every day.
2. Be grateful.
3. Eliminate toxic substances from your diet such as alcohol, drugs, cigarettes, acidic foods, and sugars.
4. Tell the truth. And this also means not disclosing information in order to mislead another person.
5. Stop leading others on <u>right now</u>. If you have no intention of having a relationship with someone else, or your intention is that it is only a tempo rary relationship, let them know immediately.
6. Stop all forms of gossip, including listening to gossip. If you are completely conscious, you can rely on your own judgment of another rather than having to learn about them by from second-hand information.
8. Take care of your body.

9. Follow through with what you say you are going to do. If you invite some one out to dinner, follow through. If you tell someone you will get back to them, do so. Again, this goes under the category of integrity and honesty.
10. Be present in every interaction with another living soul.
11. Be present with yourself.

Being truthful is the quickest way to raise your vibrational level. Every lie we tell causes a fracture in our energy system, and a fracture in the energy system will result in spiritual leaks. Just like leaks in a roof cause damage to a house over time, leaks to our energy system cause damage to the soul.

In his book *Power Vs. Force,* David R. Hawkins, M.D., Ph.D., says the following: "Ignorance does not yield to attack but it dissipates in the light, and nothing dissolves dishonesty faster than the simple act of revealing the truth. The only way to enhance one's power in the world is by increasing one's integrity, understanding, and capacity for compassion. If the diverse populations of mankind can be brought to this realization the survival of human society and the happiness of its members secure."

Another way to raise your vibrations is to be mindful of what you are subjecting yourself to on a daily basis. Do you watch PBS programming, or do you watch programs filled with violence, degradation to women, or mindless entertainment? What kind of movies do you see? All forms of entertainment have an energy level and if you want to raise your energy level and attract people into your life then the fastest way to do this is to stop filling your senses with entertainment that is violent in nature or pornographic. This is another form of spiritual abuse.

What thoughts, feelings and words are you using about yourself and others right now, in this moment? Say, "I am love. I create love. I attract love in all that I do, say, think, feel, and hear."

I once had the opportunity to go to Paris. I saw beauty everywhere I went. When my son and I became lost, we walked into a pastry shop where the clerk gave my son a chocolate éclair for free and offered me directions. I saw so many lovely things in France and was greeted with warmth and kindness by the people. Why? Because my thoughts during my time in France were: "I am love. I create love. I attract love wherever I go."

Believe and know with absolute certainty that you are love and you radiate love. Love will come to you in waves. Remember: Like attracts like.

I've always had an intense connection to dolphins and wanted someday to study them. When I was nineteen I had the opportunity to study with Dr. John Lilly in Kauai, Hawaii. Dr. Lilly is a well-known scientist recognized for his research into communicating with dolphins by translating language from human to dolphin and vice versa.

During this time, members of the team would go out on a boat in search of dolphins. Day after day, people came back complaining that they would see the dolphins but the dolphins wouldn't come near the boat. Because I had a fear of being in a boat in the middle of the ocean, I stayed on land.

I remember this clearly. After he listened to the complaints, Dr. Lilly looked over at me, and then back at the group and said, "Take Susan and the dolphins will show up."

You can imagine how I felt about that! I was not a happy camper. I said I didn't want to go, to which Dr. Lilly replied, "Do you want bliss?"

"Sure, who doesn't?" I said.

"Go out on the damn boat and you'll find it," he said.

Well, with everyone staring at me, I realized if I didn't go, there would be a lot of people mad at me! So I went. Wrapped in a life vest and clinging to the bench in the center of the boat, I went. After a while I heard people shouting that a pod of dolphins were near the boat and were coming closer.

People began to dive into the water. I stayed on my perch until I saw dolphins surround the boat, jumping out of the water. Someone yelled, "Come on, jump in!"

I took off the life vest and jumped into the ocean. Dolphins surrounded me, and I felt that it was as though they knew intuitively how frightened I was. One dolphin swam close to my side. She was so close, I was able to reach out and touch her. At the moment of contact with her, my fear dissolved and I swam as if it were second nature to me.

I dove down into the water and saw a baby dolphin swimming toward me. He stopped right in front of me and stared.

It was the first time I had ever felt total and complete bliss in my life. The feeling of freedom was so overwhelming that everything I do now in my life is to have the experience of that freedom again. This freedom seems to elude most human beings. With this true freedom, there are no bonds. There is only joy and honor of yourself and of others.

Remember that you are divine. When you become aware of this, you move toward freedom. And you choose to see beauty wherever you go.

dolphin visualization

Lie down in a comfortable place.

Soften.

Picture a calm, inviting ocean.

See the turquoise blue of the waves. Hear the sounds, feel the warmth of the water as you swim gracefully in the water.

In the distance you see three dolphins approaching you. They smile and invite you into their circle.

See yourself as a dolphin. Feel the freedom of gliding through the waves with ease.

Feel the connection to the other three as you play and communicate with each other.

You are free.

Fly through the waves. Feel the joy of being in connection with the ocean.

Know that in this and every moment you are as free as a dolphin.

You are born for bliss. Release all unrewarding beliefs. See them dissolve like foam on the sand.

All bad habits dissolve on the beach.

That's right, let them go.

Be free. Life is your playground meant to be lived to the fullest.

Live free like the dolphin.

journal page

Date: _____

Name the times when you were fearful of doing something but did it anyway. How did you feel about yourself afterward?

Make a list of the times when you've been stuck in a seemingly "impossible" situation and had an insight as to how to get unstuck.

chapter ten

HOW TO BE A MASTER ATTRACTOR

There have been many masters of attraction: Cleopatra, Marilyn Monroe, JFK, Bill Clinton, and too many others to mention here. We have all met people who radiate charisma the moment they step into a room. Oprah Winfrey is a master attractor. The woman has such a magnetic energy field that people are drawn to her.

Your greatest teachers are master attractors. Think of some of the best teachers you've had. You wanted to learn from them, and you did!

If you look closely at the attributes they share, the one that stands out the most is charisma. All of the people mentioned here exude charisma to the degree that most people who have been in their presence say they have been completely awed.

Another trait shared by a master attractor is the ability to make you feel as if you are the only person in their universe. You are captivated by them and hypnotized by their personality. The master attractor often has an air of mystery about him. You soon come to realize that he knows almost everything about you, yet you may know very little about him.

This is because people who want to know all about you become irresistible.

Master attractors are great listeners. Think of all the bores you've met at parties or functions. What's the one thing they share in common? They talk about nothing but themselves.

In order to create an air of mystery, it's vital to be a little bit elusive. People want what they can't have. And if they can have you whenever they want you, or if you are completely available to them, then you lose your mystery.

If you want a particular person to notice you, you must make them aware of your existence. If you are too shy or nervous to make your approach, then try the following exercise.

Think of someone you know who exudes confidence or sex appeal. It can be anyone – a friend, a celebrity, a pop star – anyone who you are certain would be completely confident in approaching the person you want to talk to.

If you are a woman, let's use Halle Berry as an example. She's beautiful, smart, and confident. Now pretend you jump into Halle Berry's body and you become her. Feel the confidence spread though you. How would you speak?

How does that situation look to you now? Walk across the room as if you are Halle Berry. Good! Now with this strategy in mind, go up to the person you want to speak to and address him/her with confidence. Before you talk to this person, know what you are going to say. Have an outcome. Know what you want before going into a conversation.

If you are a man, see yourself jump into George Clooney's body. Wow, how does that feel? What would you sound like if you spoke like George? Would you speak with confidence? Yes. And if you are speaking to a woman, give her certainty. Women crave certainty from a man. Already know what you want before entering into the conversation with her.

Find out about her, her needs and dreams. Have an intention for the conversation.

Master attractors almost always have a back-up plan. If someone turns them down flat, they ask out someone else. Master attractors seem to be people who can weather any storm. They also come up with option after option. They never become boxed in by self-doubt or failure. And they look at failure as an opportunity to gather even more success. Master attractors fill a room with their presence. They seem to almost glow with an inner light. There is something god- or goddess-like about them.

You are the master attractor.

Say to yourself: "I am a master attractor. I exude charisma. I am magnetic. Everywhere I go, people are attracted to me, they don't know why, they just are."

Before you go out for your day, see a golden light surround you. Now let this light expand and grow until it fills the room. Let this golden glowing light fill your living space. See it pulsing, vibrating. Now say, "I am a master attractor!"

Everywhere you go, fill the room with your presence. People won't be able to resist you.

There are other "tricks" master attractors use to be irresistible. They always look their best. One thing that stood out to me when I went to Madrid recently was how great everyone looked. I tried to pinpoint what it was. After speaking with a Spanish woman, she told me that when Spanish children are young, they learn to be groomed before going out. They are clean, their nails are well manicured, their hair is styled, and they always look put together. They also keep their bodies fit and toned.

To stay ahead of the game and be presentable doesn't take a lot of money, either. As far as clothes go, find a magazine that has outfits put together that you like and find a similar outfit. Start to exercise daily. It doesn't matter if it's walking around your neighborhood or joining a gym. Move your body. When you move your body, you create energy and energy attracts!

Stay away from destructive substances. Over-consumption of alcohol is very destructive to the physical body and psyche. It drains your energy and keeps you in a de-evolved state. I had a challenge where I was drinking too much wine. Any time I became stressed, I'd drink wine at night to fall asleep and to get into another state. As a result, I gained weight and became depressed.

One night I dreamt of my grandfather who had been dead for twelve years. In the dream, I saw myself sitting in a chair in a dark room. I could hear wind all around me and then it became silent. My grandfather entered the room and I remember the joy I felt at seeing him again. He held out his hand and I took it. Together we walked side by side in silence. I could feel the love and strength pouring out of him into me. He stopped walking, looked at me and said, "I'm always by your side; you are not alone." Then he vanished.

The dream continued and I saw myself at a party where everyone appeared out of control and drunk. A woman handed me a glass or wine and before drinking it, I looked inside the glass and saw a black liquid with mold on the surface and mold all around the sides of the glass. I threw down the glass and left the party without a backward glance.

The next day I called an NLP counselor I know and after a twenty minute session to clean up any residual addiction patterns to wine, I knew I was over it.

I have not had a glass of wine or alcohol since, nor have I wanted one.

If you smoke, stop. <u>Do whatever it takes</u> to quit and do it today. If you take illegal substances, stop. Pick up the phone and call a counselor, or find a 12-step program. They are listed in the phone book. Call information and get the number for Alcoholics Anonymous. They will be able to direct you to a Narcotic Anonymous meeting. Go today. Call right <u>now</u>.

Get mad. Do it <u>now</u>. If food is your addiction, they have Overeaters Anonymous. Go to a meeting. Find a Weight Watchers or NutriSystem <u>and join</u>. Find a Jazzercise place and sign up. I love it. I've made many wonderful friendships in Jazzercise. Do it today.

The key to breaking a pattern or addiction is <u>sustained action</u>. It takes thirty days to create a habit, and thirty days to break one.

journal page

Date: _____

What habits do you have that you'd like to not have?

What step can you take to let go of the habit?

What would you do if you weren't doing the habit? What else could you do?

chapter eleven

GET IN TOUCH WITH YOUR SUBCONSCIOUS THROUGH YOUR DREAMS

You can solve problems during sleep by programming yourself to awaken at any hour. I do this on a regular basis. You can program yourself to lose weight while you are asleep and you can leave your body during sleep. The potential of the human mind is infinite. We have only begun to know our capabilities, much less apply them. There has been much research done showing that the "I" or the ego can (and does) leave the body while you are asleep.

In sleep we are more conscious than we are "awake."

The Aborigines of Australia call it "dream time." They know the connection between the subconscious and the conscious is bridged through dreams. They also know that when a person is asleep their astral body travels out of the physical body to far-off places and through time, both into the past and the future.

The astral body is connected to the physical body by an energy cord. This energy cord is similar to the umbilical of a newborn. In sleep we visit friends and loved ones, whether they are here on the physical plane or in spirit on the astral plane. Through lucid dreaming, we program our dreams to accomplish what it is that we want to attract in our lives.

So if you want to attract a mate into your life, write down what kind of person you want, all the attributes you want this person to have. Remember the exercise in Chapter Two? Go back to it if you need a refresher.

How do you want this person to be in a relationship with you? Emotionally available? Sensitive, a great listener, a radically honest person? Someone who is spiritual? All of these things and more?

Write down exactly what you want in a mate.

Now visualize this person. How do you want them to look? How do you want them to be physically? What kind of physical relationship do you want? Do you want a long distance relationship or not? Write it all down.

When you have it down on paper – the mate you want to attract - draw this person on a blank sheet of paper. Even if you can't draw, make a sketch. Now have it fixed in your mind the kind of person you want to be in a relationship with. See yourself interacting with this person in a positive and loving way. See the person smiling at you, happy to be with you.

What are you saying to each other? Create the dialogue you will have with this person. What kinds of things do you do together? See yourself interacting with this person.

Now see yourself holding the other person surrounded with love and energy. Freeze this picture and turn it into a still photo. Take the photo and gently toss it into your near future.

And say to yourself, "When I fall asleep, my astral body will find my mate. My mate is now aware of me and is traveling through time to find me and we will meet and share a life together." You are programming your subconscious mind to find your mate. You are sending out a signal, a flare for the other person's subconscious to pick up and follow. Do this every night before you go to sleep. You are setting up for yourself the very things you are asking for.

The movie *What the Bleep Do We Know* explains how we create our reality through our thoughts. It shows how a woman continually attracts negative experiences into her life and we see why. She is filled with anger and bitterness, and she hates herself. It is only when she is shown by a child that she understands that her thoughts are creating her life. It is only after she realizes the beauty of her soul and begins to love her life that her thoughts change. Thus her life changes for the better.

Have you ever known someone who always seems to have "bad" things happen to them? Take notice of their language pattern and you will see that they attract negative situations into their life. Language patterns reflect what a person's thoughts are. If you listen well, people tell you who they are.

If a man tells you he doesn't want to be in a committed relationship, believe him. If a woman tells you she has always been the one to end a relationship, believe her.

Both of these types of people are telling you who they are. They are letting you know they are incapable of true intimacy. They are letting you know they value their ego more than their higher self. So where do you think you would be in their life? That's right, pretty low. And as long as you are meeting their needs and expectations, and feeding their egos, they will keep you in their lives...until they find someone else who feeds their ego better, and according to their rules.

I was in a relationship that was a continual source of pain. The person wasn't right for me but I stubbornly hung on, refusing to listen to friends and family members who warned me. I refused to listen even though I knew in my heart he wasn't right for me. He lied continually, took advantage of me financially, and was an emotional abuser. I had to face the reality that I allowed all of this to happen. No one can use you unless on some level you have given them permission to do so.

Subconsciously, I began to work on letting go of this person. I visualized the two of us together and I saw us thanking each other for the lessons we gave each other. I saw us giving one another a hug. I saw myself telling him goodbye, and walking away happy that it happened and happy with the knowledge that the next person I met would love me abundantly and would have all the qualities and values I wanted in a mate. With this intent in mind, I went to sleep and that night I dreamt of the person I'd said goodbye to. In the dream we were good friends and shared a mutual love and respect for one another.

When I woke up the next morning, the pain I felt disappeared. When I thought of this person, I was happy for him and in the knowledge that it was finished.

My subconscious became my healer. All I had to do was state what I wanted – not what I didn't want because I didn't want to attract what I did not want. Remember to state what you want with clarity.

journal page

Date: _____

List the following:

What do I want?

Am I certain I want this with every fiber of my being? Why? What will it give me when I have it?

dream exercise

Buy a journal or spiral notebook. Set it, along with a pen, next to your bed. Begin writing down every dream you have. If you find you can't seem to remember your dreams, simply write down the feeling of the dream. As you write the dream, ask yourself questions: "Is there something I need to become aware of?" "What do I need to bring into my conscious awareness at this moment in time?"

My friend Joan does her dream journaling right after she gets up. If not, her mind forgets her dreams as her day's "To Do" list intrudes.

There is a part of us that wants to hang onto a problem even though the answer is right in front of our faces and is available to us at any time. That part is the ego.

When you find yourself in a dilemma and unable to find a solution, ask yourself the question, "Will I continue to be a hostage of my ego, or am I willing to be a master communicator with my soul and solve this challenge right now?"

Know that the ego is like a troop of monkeys that run wild in the forest, creating disruption and causing mischief wherever they go.

Morning Intention

- Today my subconscious and conscious mind work and play together in perfect harmony.
- Any challenge that arises, I welcome, for I know the solution has also arisen and is readily available to me whenever I want.

Night Intention

- Tonight my unconscious mind will give me the answer to what I need to know in this moment in time.

My intention is _____.

Whatever you need to know regarding your intention will come to you as you sleep. When you awaken in the morning feeling refreshed, happy and more youthful, you will intuitively know the steps to take to achieve your intention.

When you wake up, write down everything you remember about your dreams. Write the colors, the sounds you heard, the sensations, the people. Describe every single thing, no matter how inconsequential you may think it is.

Also, write down any words spoken in the dream that comes to you.

Do this without editing or pausing. Use no periods, commas, nothing that will infringe on the writing process.

Write for fifteen minutes.

Go!

chapter twelve

WHAT ARE YOUR TEN GOALS FOR A RELATIONSHIP?

TOP 10 RELATIONSHIP GOALS

Goal#	Goal	Date
1.		
2.		
3.		
4.		
5.		
6.		
7.		
8.		
9.		
10.		

TOP 10 VALUES YOU WANT IN A MATE

Top 10 Values for a Mate and Why

1.

2.

3.

4.

5.

6.

7.

8.

9.

10.

chapter thirteen

WHAT KIND OF PERSON DO YOU REALLY WANT?

Let's really get to the core of the kind of person you want to attract. In the space below, write 50 things you absolutely want in a mate. Honesty? Trust? Humor? Communication? Write down everything you can think of. Everything!

1.
2.
3.
4.
5.
6.
7.
8.
9.
10.
11.
12.
13.
14.
15.
16.

17.

18.

19.

20.

21.

22.

23.

24.

25.

26.

27.

28.

29.

30.

31.

32.

33.

34.

35.

36.

37.

38.

39.

40.

41.

42.

43.

44.

45.

46.

47.

48.

49.

50.

What kind of person are you willing to become in order to attract your ideal mate?

Write down the 50 things in a mate you absolutely will not tolerate. Smoking? Drinking? Emotional issues? Humorlessness? Lying? Think of everything you can that you will absolutely not tolerate.

1.
2.
3.
4.
5.
6.
7.
8.
9.
10.
11.
12.
13.
14.
15.
16.
17.
18.
19.
20.
21.
22.
23.

24.

25.

26.

27.

28.

29.

30.

31.

32.

33.

34.

35.

36.

37.

38.

39.

40.

41.

42.

43.

44.

45.

46.

47.

48.

49.

50.

THE FINAL ASSESSMENT AND PLANNING FOR ATTRACTING THE LOVE YOU WANT INTO YOUR LIFE

As you have assimilated what you want and removed any of the old fears about relationships, you will begin to see a transformation take place in your life. Before leaving this chapter, make a plan for how you want to begin to attract love into your life.

1. My strengths are:

2. When I am in a relationship, I am this way to my partner:

3. How I want my partner to be in a relationship:

4. If there are any boundaries in my energy field, what are they and how can I resolve them quickly:

5. My goals for a relationship are:

The best way to break a destructive pattern is through sustained action. I make a commitment to take the following actions:

I make a commitment to:

chapter fourteen

HOW TO INSTILL NEW BELIEFS INTO YOUR FUTURE

First let us decide what new beliefs you have. Do you want the belief that you are worthy of unconditional love? Do you want to believe that you will have the relationship of your dreams? Do you want to believe that you are charismatic and that right now you are drawing this person into you life? Any or all of those beliefs are possible, or any beliefs that you choose.

Remember to tell yourself: I am worthy of unconditional love. I am one with the infinite flow of love from my heart and soul. I am love, and I am loved, cherished, and honored by the love of my life. Love flows to me constantly and love flows from me constantly. I am attracting the relationship of my dreams right now. Charisma sparkles all around me and I am now drawing in the right love into my life right now.

Now write down the new beliefs in the following space. Look at what you have written and say the beliefs out loud.

After you have said your beliefs at least four times, picture yourself being and living the beliefs. See yourself flowing with love. See yourself in the relationship of your dreams. Good! Now feel the feelings of being in this amazing relationship. Hear the sounds. See yourself exuding charisma. Once you see all of this, capture it on a card in you mind. Now take this snapshot along with other beliefs you want such a spirituality, blissful living, prosperity, and put each one of these new beliefs about yourself on the card and gently toss the card into the present, sending it into your future.

Live from this moment on as if you already have all of those things. Live like you are exuding charisma. Live, love, and be loved.

journal page

Date: _____

Know that you are love. People fall in love with you wherever you go. The love of your life is here for you.

Take the time to write about your life with the love of your life in it. What does this life look like? How do you sound together? How does it feel?

chapter fifteen

HOW TO PREPARE FOR LOVE TO ENTER YOUR NET

Continue to work on clearing your energy systems. Work on this at least fifteen minutes each day. Don't forget to avoid destructive substances and situations. Avoid being addicted to being right all the time.

Take care of you, your body, and your emotional and mental health. Have absolute respect for your life and for the lives of others. Know and honor how special you are. If someone doesn't know and honor how special you are, bless that person out of your life and move on. A person who has no respect for himself or others will not have respect for you.

Check your beliefs again. Is your belief that you are worthy of love an unshakeable one? Yes? Good! Repeat every day, "I am worthy of unconditional love. I attract unconditional love into my life every moment I am alive." Say this every day because the more you repeat this, the more firmly this belief will show up in your life.

Make it a habit to not dwell on the past. Don't blame the past for current challenges. Go forward with the knowledge that you have experienced the past relationships to make you stronger. Past experiences, negative or positive, are gifts. Negative experiences can be transformed into present and future victories because of your new beliefs.

Our biggest lessons in life are our mistakes, and rather than waste time regretting something we did or what someone else did to us, let's say, "Next time it will be different!" Now you know what kind of person or circumstances to stay away from. You had to go through what you did to get to where you are today.

Saints aren't born overnight. Saints, great teachers, healers, all get to where they are by trials and tribulations. The thing they have in common is that they will not wallow in regret or self-pity. They move on and continue their mission, whatever it is.

You are on a mission. Your mission is to be in a loving relationship and to be surrounded by loving friends. Nothing will stop you from this. Continue to see yourself in loving relationships, put your thoughts in alignment with thoughts of love. See yourself with the love of your life, see and feel how your thoughts and the other person's thoughts reach each other in perfect harmony.

See and feel yourself perceiving the real you in yourself and in the other person. See and feel the other person perceiving the real you. Know that you both are in deep communication with each other on both a conscious and a subconscious level.

Close your eyes and imagine your hand on the other person's heart and that person's hand on yours. Feel each other's heartbeat. Hear the sound of both of your hearts beating.

What do you know about this other person? What does your heart say? Speak it out loud. Write it down and keep it with you.

You decide what you want to experience. Practice choosing good and loving experiences for yourself. Know what you are experiencing. You have chosen on some level to experience it.

Practice being aware of the experiences you are choosing. What are your thoughts right now? Good thoughts or fearful ones? We attract what we fear the most. If you are constantly focused on fear-based thoughts such as being afraid of terrorists or some kind of disaster you will attract the exact opposite of what you want.

Love is the opposite of fear. A person with fear-based thoughts will not attract love into their life. They will constantly keep it at arm's length.

Energy follows attention, so look at where you are directing your attention. Go inside of yourself for a moment. Where is your attention? What thoughts are you experiencing?

Know that you are a great person capable of achieving anything you put your mind to. You have a brain, a consciousness, and a spirit that is eternal. You are in control of your mind – not the other way around. You have the ability to direct your life as you want.

Do you know what you want your outcome to be? Do you want a life partner? Do you want to be married? Do you want a monogamous relationship? Live in separate places?

Decide and know what it is you want.

What are you like in relationships? What will you be like? Is there anything you need to change to experience a total relationship?

exercise

Stay in a positive state to attract a positive person. If you happen to fall back into an old unworkable pattern, do the following exercise. Ask yourself these questions and write down the answers.

- Can you remember a time when you felt totally happy?

- Can you remember a time when you felt totally excited?

- Can you remember a time when you felt totally loved?

- Can you remember a time when you laughed out loud?

- Can you remember a time when you felt completely confident?

Now go back to each one of those times and experience them fully. Write about each one on the following pages.

happy

excited

laughed out loud

completely confident

What are your thoughts now after doing the exercise? Did you experience a change in your reality when you thought of all the good things that have happened to you?

What happens to us and how we perceive it is what we make of it.

I can think of a past relationship and pick out all the bad things that happened and I get bad feelings about it. Or, I can think of a past relationship and pull up all the good things that happened and I can have good feelings about it.

I have taught myself to understand that when a relationship ends that the next person I meet and the next relationship I am in will be a trillion times better than any previous relationship.

And you know what? That really works. The relationship I am in now is a trillion times better than any previous relationship I have ever been in. When I am with Jim either physically or on the phone, I simply remember the most amazing feeling I have ever had with him and I intensify that feeling.

Know that thoughts are living things far more powerful than we can ever measure. Know that you are forever.

"For here, where there is neither past nor future, the doors of perception are cleared, and we see everything as it is — infinite."
Alan Watts

chapter sixteen

MOVE YOUR BODY

If you want to meet someone, it's important to get yourself out there into the world. People meet people at work, health clubs, doing volunteer work, taking classes, joining a club, or by going to seminars. The point is to get your body to move. Allow others the privilege of experiencing your vibrancy.

You are a beautiful, elegant soul. Give others the opportunity to see and feel your energy. People want you in their lives. Share the universe's gift that is you.

exercise

List all the places you can go to meet other people.

- Continue to grow by reading and by attending personal growth seminars.
- Go to a church, temple or place of worship. Be of service to people in need.
- Walk a couple of times per day.
- Meditate to restore balance.
- Listen to soothing music.
- Speak in a way you wouldn't normally speak. Try using an English or French accent and have fun with it!
- Look up and smile.
- Meet one new person every day and find out about them. Listen to them intently without speaking. Really try to understand that person.
- Paint a picture.
- Look into the mirror and smile.
- Walk barefoot outside in the grass.
- Sing out loud.

journal page

Date: _____

List ways in which you can move your body.

Exercise and what type:
Running
Walking alone or with a friend
Dancing
Jazzercise

_____
_____
_____
_____
_____
_____
_____
_____
_____
_____
_____

When are you going to choose to move your body into a peak state through exercise?

chapter seventeen

FEMININE AND MASCULINE ENERGY

Each of us has both feminine and masculine energy available to us. Sometimes there can be an imbalance. For example, a man can use his masculine energy from a fear base.

A man who operates from fear will be controlling, abusive, achievement-oriented, addicted to substances and sex, addicted to fantasies and masturbation, afraid of intimacy, afraid of commitment, and possibly unfaithful in a relationship.

A woman who operates from fear will have her own set of problems. Her behaviors will include: controlling, submissive, passive-aggressive, angry, bitter, gossipy, selfish, addicted to the rescue fantasy, living through others, a pleaser, depressed, emotionally unstable, addicted to substances and/or shopping.

A man living in healthy masculine energy will be loving, kind and focused; have inner strength and wisdom; want intimacy and be unafraid of commitments; be addiction-free; be the rock for his woman when she is encountering a storm; provide for himself and others. He will have a higher mission.

If you are a man, give women certainty. Take charge and be focused. If you want this woman, let her know. Women crave certainty. Give them exactly that. If you say you are going to call her, then call. If you say you are going to take her to dinner, then do it.

A woman living in healthy feminine energy will be free and happy; able to support herself; kind, loving; unafraid to be alone; be addiction-free; and know that what she gets herself into she can rescue herself from. When her man is going through a storm, she will be there beside him, giving him her full support and love.

If you are a woman, revel in your feminine energy. Men can't resist a woman who is free and acts like a feminine woman. Women, men need your appreciation. Show them you appreciate what they do for you and tell them so.

If you are still playing games, stop it now. You will attract another game player with "player" being the operative word. Recognize when someone is playing games with you.

The following are some signs that the person might not be sincere:

- They say they will call and they don't.
- They play hard to get.
- They invite you to dinner and don't follow through.
- They break promises and apologize, only to do it again.
- They make no move to take the relationship to the next level.
- They show up when it's convenient for them.
- Instead of certainty, they consistently give you uncertainty.

Work on expanding your consciousness. Fill a room with your energy before you enter it. Think big, taking comfort in knowing that you can attract the love you desire into your life.

There's a story that illustrates the perfect point about thinking big.
Arnold Palmer was teaching the King of Saudi Arabia how to play golf. At the end of the lessons, the king told Mr. Palmer he wanted to give him a gift. Mr. Palmer politely refused saying it had been an honor to teach golf to the king.

The king persisted and asked Mr. Palmer what he liked. Mr. Palmer responded that he collected golf clubs, to which the king replied that he would send him one. Back home, the days passed and Mr. Palmer wondered what sort of golf club he would receive from the king. Would it be engraved with his name? Would it have precious jewels embedded in it? He wondered and waited.

Then one day, a courier arrived at Mr. Palmer's house and handed him an envelope. When Mr. Palmer opened it, he saw it was a gift from the king – a deed to a 160-acre private golf club.

Kings think bigger! Think like a king or queen and watch your world expand. Watch the people who begin to enter your life.

While you are waiting, be grateful for what you have in your life now. If you believe in God or a higher power, then show your gratitude by being your higher self every day.

Be grateful for the love that comes into your life.

Be the best you can be mentally, emotionally, spiritually, and physically. Live your dream and your dream will become our life.

king exercise for men

You are a king. Think like a king. Feel the feelings of a king. Picture yourself as a glorious king and hear your words. Write down what you will accomplish as a king.

My first year as a King I will:

Within the next five years as a King I will:

Within the next ten years as a King I will:

Within the next twenty-five years as a King I will:

My legacy as a King is:

queen exercise for women

You are a queen. Think like a queen. Feel the feelings of a queen. Picture yourself as a glorious queen and hear your words. Write down what you will accomplish as a queen.

My first year as a Queen I will:

Within the next five years as a Queen I will:

Within the next ten years as a Queen I will:

Within the next twenty-five years as a Queen I will:

My legacy as a Queen is:

chapter eighteen

COMMUNE WITH **YOUR CORE**

Know that you are in constant communication with your core. As you become more aware and more conscious, day by day and moment by moment, you will begin to see that your communication is a continuing awareness of a deep connection between your soul and the souls of others. Opportunities will flourish. Coincidences will occur on a regular basis.

Have faith that your dreams will come true and have patience. Impatient people are selfish people.

Everything has its own rhythm, its own pattern. The key is to stay in constant communication with your core rhythm. The better you know yourself the easier it will be to know when the right person will come into your life. Jesus says, "If only you had the faith of a mustard seed."

A mustard seed is a tiny seed that when placed in even a harsh arid environment, it will grow and flourish into a huge tree. The mustard seed knows what it is capable of, and fulfills its destiny against all odds. So can you. Know with complete certainty that you are love and love flows through you and to you in complete abundance just like that mustard seed can grow.

Commune with your soul by becoming still. Meditate for a few moments or for a long time. You can meditate anywhere, any time, and in any circumstance. Relax and allow your mind to be quiet. "Listen" to your spirit. What is it saying to you?

Milton Erickson, famed therapist and master hypnotist, decided he wanted to be able to fall asleep anywhere, even in the loudest places. He found a factory that made metal parts. The noise created there was so loud that the workers had to wear earplugs to deafen the noise. He asked the owner if he could stay there and try to sleep. The owner was more amused than anything and told him yes. After three days Milton Erickson trained himself to fall asleep and to stay asleep in those adverse conditions!

The human mind can be trained to do and believe anything.

Think like the genius that you are. Believe you are a beacon of love that gushes forth love and recycles it back to you, and your life will be filled with love.

Love energy transforms lower energy patterns. Once you become transformed by love your energy will shift. You will see an increase in your vibrational levels, and you will attract others with high vibrations.

Have you ever looked at someone or touched someone and felt a lightening bolt pass through you? This is because of the electricity that has been exchanged between the two of you. You have a spark for someone, an instant chemistry. Sometimes these attractions are sexually based, and the relationship is primarily a sexual relationship that runs its course after a while.

You want to feel that spark for someone, that electrical charge. You also want a complete connection that serves both of your needs, including spiritual and emotional needs. This kind of relationship will bring you bliss. A relationship with that "spark" is like a thunderbolt which is created when a cloud gets enough particles to charge one way, and the earth has enough particles to charge the other way.

The spark between two people is created much the same way because we are vats of energy. When a part of us is on the same wavelength as another person, and these two people pass one another, they will feel a spark.

journal page

Date: _____

Sometimes we feel a physical attraction or a spark for someone, get into a relation-ship with that person, and soon realize it was a mistake. Has this happened to you? How many times? Did you grow from this experience?

Can you have a spark for another person and share the same values? What are some ways you can discover the other person's values to determine if he/she is the right person for you?

chapter nineteen

ACTIVATE YOUR POWERFUL MAGICAL NET

If there is some relaxing instrumental music you like, please turn it on now.

Lie down in a comfortable area and be completely relaxed. Begin to take deep, slow rhythmic breaths. Allow your body and mind to relax into a quiet state of being.

Breathe in, breath out.

Now tighten your feet and relax them.
Good.

Go up your legs and tighten your leg muscles and release.

Tighten your glutes and release.

Take a deep breath and tighten your stomach muscles.
That's right.

Now square your fists, and relax your hands, stretching out your fingers. Squeeze your shoulders, and relax.

Breath deep, exhale, tighten your face and relax.

Picture in your mind that warm healing oil is pouring over your scalp. This oil is slowly pouring over and into your mind and body.

You are like the oil, fluid and warm and free.

Breathing in, exhale.

Now see the cells in your stomach area within the core of your being.

These cells are moving, dancing, swirling around within you.

Feel the energy within your core. Hear the sounds. What does it sound like?

See this energy in the center of your belly. It is the essence of your core.

See it swirling around, and around, each tiny powerful, healthy molecule, alive, vibrating with intensity.

The molecules and cells create colors: amethyst purples, rose pinks, tangerines, vivid yellows, and shimmering gold. As these colors swirl and gain velocity, they create charisma and emotions, feelings of love, perfect health and acceptance.

Each cell, each color, makes a special sound. This sound is made for the one to hear, for the one to answer the call of your soul.

Now, these colors, feelings, and sounds form a living stream and like a geyser, this powerful stream bursts out of you belly button and takes shape.

The shape turns into a beautiful glowing net that undulates and unfolds like a wave.

See the colors – iridescent, changing, glowing. Feel the vibrations of your net as it pulses with energy, resonating with your spirit, aligning with your mission.

Now say the following:

I love and accept myself fully. I am continually growing emotionally and spiritually.

I am ready and emotionally available for love to come into my life.

My heart is ready.
My spirit is welcoming of love.

The net now manifests for me the love of my dreams and the friendships that are harmonious.

Love I attract into my life is emotionally available for me.

Breathe in, exhale.

Let your net unfold, for the net travels far and wide. It covers every inch of the earth with love. You will suddenly find that wherever you go, wherever your spirit and body travel, people fall in love with you. With love, they are healed. They gain sudden insights and epiphanies spring into their consciousness by your presence. There is something about you that draws them close to you. Something undefined about you that soothes their souls.

Your energy opens their eyes to the truth.

The net works in alignment with other nets. If your friend's love falls into your net, your net flicks this love back into your friend's net.

If a flounder jumps into your net, or a love that isn't right for you, your net flicks him/her out. The net has an ancient wisdom as old as time and it knows who is right and who isn't. When you activate your net, you become conscious of people who are right for you or not.

Breathe in, breathe out.

Every breath is strengthening, energizing your net.

Feel the subconscious connection to your love. Hear the sounds of both of your love's and your own heart, the energy of the two of you in divine togetherness.

Feel the connection of your souls that grows stronger with each beat of time. The attraction is undeniable, the bond unbreakable. With every breath you take, with every heartbeat, you are brought closer, closer until you are together.

Your net is flowing with love, energized and magnetized with your own net power! Only love is forever and love is the total absence of fear.

Letting go of another person is letting go of your fear of what keeping that person in your life represents.

People say to me what they really want is to be loved unconditionally. They want to have someone to love unconditionally.

Let's look at what it truly means to love someone unconditionally. If you have been in a relationship with someone and no longer are do you say: "I once loved that person but I no longer do. I love someone else now"?

If so, then you never loved them in the first place. The relationship may be over from the standpoint of the physical, emotional, and mental but if you once loved that person, you will always love them.

There are people I have loved in the past and even though I might never see them again or will never share physical intimacy with them, I will always love them.

Love doesn't "hang on" and love doesn't control another person. When you are hanging onto someone or trying to control them, you have stepped out of the realm of love and into the realm of ego.

I have been in relationships where I found myself hanging on and not letting go of the person when it was clear that the relationship was unbalanced. Upon becoming fully conscious of when a relationship is unbalanced and is no longer working, I have forgiven myself, the other person, and have let it go.

When you are in a relationship and you are unsure if it's right or you aren't clear if it's time to let go, check in with your spirit. Ask some questions.

- Are you happy in this relationship, or do you spend most of the time being unhappy?

- Is the relationship a continual source of uncertainty for you?

- How do you feel after an interaction with this person? Upset or happy?

- How do you feel before an interaction with this person? Upset, unsure, or happy?

- Are you a priority in the other person's life?

- Are they a priority in yours?

Recognizing where your emotions are in a relationship is very important. Think clearly about these questions and learn to recognize where your ego is in control. If this love is meant to be, it will happen. If not, let go so the love you are supposed to be with can enter your life.

If you are still in *any* kind of relationship with another person, you will block the love you want into your life. Clear your net of the flounders and bless them out of your life; then the golden whale or the silver dolphin can come in.

journal page

Date: _____

Assignment

Do the net visualization at night before you go to bed and in the morning when you wake up. Find a friend and do this visualization together also.

Do this for two weeks and write down your results. Do people seem to respond to you differently after doing The Net?

chapter twenty

ART OF RELEASING

When I was nineteen, one of my mother's friends gave me a baby Artic fox. The fox's mother had been killed and her pup lay near her body when she was found. She was so small she fit inside of a moccasin. She was given the name Wakeega, which means little moccasin.

My mother's friend found that he couldn't raise Wakeega because she had a habit of eating all the duck eggs around his pond. He knew I was good with animals and that I had been raised on a horse and cattle ranch, so he gave Wakeega to me.

This beautiful and unique creature proved difficult to train. Wakeega got out of her pen once and I spent hours chasing her. She seemed to delight in the fact that I could never quite catch her. She never ran completely out of my sight.

Finally, I just gave up. I lay on the grass and looked up at the sky and watched the clouds. After a few minutes I felt something next to me. When I glanced over I saw Wakeega. She had curled up beside me and fallen fast asleep. I had to learn to let her go, and she came to me.

the visualization for letting go

Find a nice area to either sit or lie down. Adjust your breathing.

Breathe in, breathe out.

Breathe in, breathe out.
That's right.

Now in your mind's eye, see the other person.

Is there an energy between you?

See this energy.

Where is it coming from?
Your heart?
Your belly?
Your head?

Locate the energy.
Find it and hear any sound it makes.
Good.

Breathe in, breathe out.
Relax.

You are doing fine. Thank the other person for having been in your life.

Thank the other person for the lessons you learned because of them. Tell them you are letting go of them with love.
Good.

Breathe in, breathe out.

Now imagine you have a pair of scissors in your hand and cut the energy cord between you and the other person. That's right. You may find that a part of the energy cord may be a little harder to cut. That's okay.

Say to yourself:
I am not cutting off the love I feel.
I am redirecting the love.

Now, cut the remaining energy cord. Watch as the other person goes out of your energy field.

Now, see yourself as your higher self, standing in front of you. See how happy and healthy you are, filled with loving energy.

Now, pick up the cord that was cut and place this cord into your higher self, wherever you feel compelled to. Let it attach from you to your higher self. Feel the flow of energy as the current pulses with your essence.

Next, step into your higher self and look around. How do you feel? What do the new higher vibrations sound like?

You are ready to attract another person who is on a higher vibratory level because your consciousness has now shifted to a higher realm.

Now imagine a bright white/blue light is entering your body, cleansing it, healing it, sweeping away any residue of negative energies.

See the light sweep through your body, heart, and mind – cleaning it, healing it, and sweeping away any residue of negative energies. See yourself growing younger with every breath you take.

Fall in love with who you are and others who love themselves will know how to fall in love with you. Be your own soul mate.

Love yourself. Your self-love will be like a magnet to "the one." Who can resist a happy, evolved, free, and love- filled person? Nobody.

People fall in love with you and they don't know why, they just do.

Now see and feel a shimmering rose pink light flowing through you, filling you with warmth and love.

Say to yourself: "I am filled with love and vitality. I am worthy of love. I am love. I am a beacon of pulsing, healing, glowing love. Everyone loves me."

journal page

Date: _____

Who do I need to let go of? For what reasons? When I am letting them go?

chapter twenty-one

KNOW YOU'RE WORTHY OF LOVE

We are born with the ability to love fully and to be fully loved. Because of programming by others' belief systems, we take on a negative self-image resulting in self-loathing.

The way to know love and to love another is to first love yourself unconditionally. Fall in love with the brilliant beautiful person that you are.

When we don't love ourselves, we set up emotional barriers that not only keep us from loving ourselves, but they affect our being aligned with our higher selves.

You're worthy of love by virtue of your being in existence. There are no accidents. You were born to discover how to love yourself. When you do this, love comes to you in waves.

The first step in learning how to love yourself is to allow yourself to realize the life you've led. Look back and know that no matter what happened, you made it through. Something inside of you held fast, regardless of any obstacles or odds seemed to be stacked against you. You made it.

Now take that part of you that survives no matter what, and see it as a small, flicking flame deep within. In your mind's eye watch as the flame inside you grows and spreads throughout your body. See bright colors of this steady fire as it builds into a strong healthy fire, a fire that flows throughout your body and burning away any and all destructive thoughts, all negative words, any kind of dislike, hatred, judgment, criticism, depression – all these things are being burned away by the fire within you, the cleansing flame that in a flash has wiped you clean of all the junk thought patterns, reducing the negativity to ash.

Take a deep breath and blow out.

In your mind's eye see a small pile of ashes in the palm of your hand. Know that this pile of ashes is all that's left of your old negative thought patterns.

Take a deep breath and blow the ashes out of your hand.

Watch as they fly away.
Breathe in Love

Sit in a comfortable position and breathe in regular, even breaths.

Soften your muscles.

Breathe in, exhale.

Picture the air you breathe in as a pale shimmering pink cloud. Breathe in the soft pink air.

Breathe it out.

Breathe in the pink cloud again and feel it as it activates the love that is within you.

Watch as this love grows inside you and flows into your veins.

Now picture your heart. See it grow with love so great that it fills the entire room with presence. With every breath you take feel the power of the love inside you and watch with each exhalation as that love spreads out into the air touching others.

Watch your heart breathe in this love, feel every cell, every molecule, every part of you breathe in love and blow it out.

That's right.

The air around you is charged with your loving presence and everywhere you go, people and all living things sense the love inside out and part of them becomes activated, releasing the love within themselves and hear the sounds of happiness as it flows across the atmosphere.

Good.

Now breathe in and out normally. Write in your journal how you felt during the exercise and how you feel now.

What are you saying to yourself? Has your tone softened? Any time a negative thought about yourself comes up, breathe it out and say, "I love you."

Write down everything about that time.

The questions below will prompt you to become clear about what it takes for you to feel loved:

- What do you say to yourself at the time you are feeling loved?
- What has to happen in order for you to feel loved?
- How will you know you are loved?
- How will being loved and knowing you deserve to be loved affect your life?
- When now can you decide to be loved?

I had the good fortune to have the best grandparents a kind could ever have. No matter how bad things were at home, I knew with total certainty that all I had to do was leave the house and go to my grandparents' home, where I would be loved unconditionally.

That feeling of being loved has always stayed with me. It's the same feeling I give out to my children, my students, and to people with whom I become involved.

The beautiful thing about giving love with no boundaries is you forget about yourself. There is a moment in time where the ego disappears and your core is connected to their core in complete harmony.

Those are the moments I live for. That is the state I strive to live in. That is the very essence of what I want you to want now in your life.

When you love someone or something else – a person, a pet, a mission, God, helping others – you transcend the bonds that you have tried to place upon yourself in the past.

Reach out with your heart and soul and by the very laws of the universe, love will reach out and grab you by the very fiber of your being. It is unavoidable.

I worked with a young woman recently. I knew she had been through a traumatic experience. She had a tough life, and was barely getting by. Her mother was a narcissist. Not only would she refuse help this girl out even though she was quite financially secure but she was also extremely emotionally cruel to her daughter.

I asked this young woman and two other girls with me if they would like to go shoe shopping. Of course they jumped at the offer! So along we went, the two girls talking about whether they wanted heels or flats, while the other girl, who I will call Whitney, sat quietly in the back seat. When we got to the shoe store, they excitedly piled out and went into the store.

The whole point of this had nothing to do with shoes. I wanted to see how Whitney would react to the experience. I watched as Whitney walked up and down the aisles, arms crossed, head angled downward, her eyes glancing at shoes and then back down at the floor.

The other two girls decided on a pair of shoes and were ready to check out.

Whitney was empty-handed. I asked her if she had found a pair of shoes she liked, to which she quickly answered no.

"So, let me make sure I am understanding this correctly because I want to be clear. You are telling me that in the biggest shoe store in the city, where there are thousands of shoes, you haven't found one singe pair that you want?" I asked.

She cleared her throat, which told me she had really found a pair but wasn't going to ask for them.

"Well, all right then, I guess I'll have to pick out a pair for you." I chose a pair of shoes that would have been great for someone who was forty, not twenty.

A look crossed her face. Both of the other girls looked horror-stricken.

I wanted to laugh at this point because to a woman, shoes are the barometer of coolness. Wear the wrong pair and your cool factor goes down a notch. Still, Whitney said nothing.

"Well, okay. If you don't get a pair of shoes, no one does."

You could have cut the tension with a butter knife. One of the other girls literally clutched her shoes close to her heart.

Whitney looked up for a split second and I saw a flash of fire in her eyes.

That's what I was waiting for!

"I did see a pair I kind of liked over there," she answered.

The two other girls actually breathed a sigh of relief.

We bought the shoes, left, and I knew intuitively how to reach her. I also knew Whitney felt unworthy of love and that she didn't love herself. Once I taught Whitney that when she loved herself, her life would literally change. On a dime, a new person emerged. She had learned to love herself first and to understand that she had wants and needs.

exercise - how to love yourself

If you have some relaxing instrumental music you like, turn it on now.
Find a place where you feel comfortable, lie down, and soften your body.

That's right.
Relax.
Breathe in,
exhale.
Breathe in,
exhale.

Become more and more conscious of every breath you take.

Now, think of something you are absolutely certain of, like the sun coming up in the morning.

Be aware of where the feeling comes from.
Notice where the picture of the sun comes up. Are there any sounds?
Good. What do they sound like?

Now, double this feeling of certainty, triple it, and quadruple it.
That's right.

See yourself in your mind standing in front of the sun.

See yourself smiling; see yourself growing happier as the rays of the sun pour into your heart.

Now on the sun, see the word **LOVE** in big bold print. See it still, and now see it moving.

Hear yourself say, "I love you."
Feel the feelings of the words as they go into the sun.

Watch as the words, "I love you," come back from the sun to you with all the strength, power, and energy of the sun.

Feel the words "I love you" as they go into your heart.

Feel the warmth of the sun as it fills you with life sustaining love.

Breathe in and smell the scents of love: a field of flowers, fresh cut grass, a new baby, your lover's chest.

Breathe in the scents of love.

Breathe in cinnamon, lavender, peppermint and sweet lemon.

Hear the music of love.

What does it sound like? Is it a chorus of angels? A single resonating tone, the voice of a beloved grandparent saying,
"I adore you"?

See the words as they appear on the surface of the sun. The words, "I adore you" move from the sun toward you and into your heart.

Feeling more and more certain you are adored with every breath you take. Feel the rays of the sun as they bathe your face and body in warmth, love, and adoration.

You can't help but smile more.

A smile blooms across your face and you see others smile at you and they don't know why, they just do.

Feel the love as it flows throughout your body.

Feel love as it cleanses every cell in your body. Feel love as it moves through your heart.

With the power of a trillion suns feel love as it pulses inside of you. Know with certainty that you are loved. Hear the words "I love you." See yourself vibrant with love and squeeze your fist.

Good.

See the sun in front of you, reach your hands out and pull it into your chest.

Breathe now the full power of love. Know that wherever you go, at all times, you are completely loved and you radiate love so that all who stand in your presence are bathed in love.

That's right.

See the colors, hear the sounds and feel the feelings of love.

Now say, while squeezing your fist,
"I am loved."

I love to listen to Jimmy Buffett. Every time I hear one of his songs, I smile. *Margaritaville* is one of my favorites.

journal page Date: _____

What are some of your favorite songs and why? Choose your top three favorite songs and write down what that song is saying to you.

chapter twenty-two

CHANGE YOUR WORDS, CHANGE YOUR REALITY

How often have you heard someone say they have bad luck in relationships? Or they keep attracting "losers?"

In the movie *What the Bleep Do We Know* there is a segment where the main character in the movie catches her husband cheating on her. Throughout the movie we see how her bitterness affects her life. She perceives that everyone is "cheating" and that life is hard. She hates herself and uses negative language patterns about herself and others. When she makes a transformation, she changes the language to positive and her life takes on a remarkable, beautiful change.

I know a woman who constantly complains that every day is a "bad" day and nothing ever "goes right" for her. And guess what? With her continuous negative talk, she attracts negative experiences into her life and won't take responsibility for the things that she allows into her life.

The more doom and gloom you profess, the more of that kind of energy you will attract. Change your language now. Begin to hear what comes out of your mouth. Do you gossip about other people? Yes, it will come back to you – for every action there is a reaction.

Negative language patterns become a habit that results in our addition to circumstances that are created as a result of the words a person uses.

One of the most challenging lessons for me in this lifetime has been to accept responsibility for everything that happens to me in my life. I know that I attract what I put out regardless of whether I am consciously aware of it.

I used to listen to every word someone said to me. Now I automatically sift for word patterns a person uses. Words that get my interest are the blame words: should, why, try, can't, and don't. When someone uses blame words frequently in their vocabulary, that's a signal to me that they aren't taking responsibility in areas of their life.

I once heard a woman say in an angry tone, "Why did I have to have such rubbish parents?"

After being around this woman for a time during a seminar, the thought flashed through my mind, "Why did your parents have such a rubbish kid?" I erased that thought and those words quickly and sent out a lot of love energy to her.

I believe we create spiritual contracts with people before we are born. For a long time, I got caught up in feeling depressed because I allowed earlier events from my childhood to run my life. When I look back, I realize now if I would have had different parents I would not have gone on the spiritual quest that I am on now.

I still make mistakes – a lot of them – and when I do, I take responsibility. I know that whatever happens to me is "my own damn fault."

The very instant you take responsibility of a situation the energy will shift. No matter what happens – you got ripped off, your lover lied and left you, a business deal went sour, your parents were abusive – whatever it was in the past, take that event, see it as a still picture, infuse it with a freezing cold breeze until you see the picture turn dimmer and dimmer.

Watch ice crystals form on the picture. Imagine you are holding a pair of tongs. Pick up the picture with the tongs and ask "How did I create this?" Listen for the answer. Say "I created this, I create this no more."

Now throw the picture across the room. See it hit the wall and shatter into a million tiny pieces. Watch as the pieces melt into the floor and dissolve.

Feel the feelings of taking responsibility for yourself from now on. Feel the feeling of strength. Know that courage is who you are from this moment on. Your soul has evolved to a higher level. Your vibrations are shifting higher and higher. Remain in this strength for the rest of your life.

In *The Hidden Messages in Water*, Emoto says, "I am particularly remember one photograph. It was the most beautiful and delicate crystal that I had so far seen formed by beings exposed to the words "love and gratitude." It was as if the water had rejoiced and celebrated by creating a flower in bloom. It was so beautiful that I can say that it actually changed my life from that moment on. In Japan, it is said that words of the soul reside in a spirit called Kotodama or the spirit of words, and the act of speaking words has the power to change the world."

journal page

Date: _____

List all the negative words and phrases you want to eliminate from your vocabulary. What positive words and phrases can you replace them with?

chapter twenty-three

THE **LAW** OF **JUICY ATTRACTION**

Ever hear the phrases, "Like attracts like," "Water seeks its own level," or "Birds of a feather flock together"? We have all heard those statements at some time or other in our lives.

Show me the person a man or a woman spends the most time with and I will be able to tell you what kind of person that man or woman is.

According to my friend Joan Rhine, one of the best negotiators I've ever met, "I can tell what kind of person someone is by knowing the kind of people that person associates with." If someone primarily hangs around with negative, foul-mouthed people who defile their bodies, that person is likely to be the same. Conversely, if a person gravitates toward people who are positive, who love themselves and others, the person is most likely to have those same radiant character traits.

My first job was at the age of seven when I helped my grandfather, who owned a newspaper. I would stand on a wooden box and change ink from the press. Of course, I had help from the adults but I took my job seriously and kept at it until I no longer needed any help.

Working at my grandfather's paper, the opportunity to meet and observe some of the writers and reporters who worked there came up. At around the age of eight, I decided I wanted to become a writer. Even though I knew I would most likely go into business, my dream was to write. I was already associating with writers.

The cool thing about attracting people with similar energy patterns as us is that we do it at an unconscious level. For a long time I attracted into my life people who were achievers, hard workers and people whose top value was success.

If someone entered my life who didn't have a similar work ethic as I did, they didn't stay in my life for long. I had no conscious awareness that this was going on. The challenge, although I attracted high achievers, was to be clear about the values I wanted because I was also attracting men who were materialistic, shallow, void of spirituality, and who did not know how to be intimate with another human being.

The key to the law of attraction is to be absolutely clear about what kind of person you want to attract into your life.

The other element is to be other-involved rather than be self-involved. To be self-involved is to be insecure, and insecurity attracts an insecure mate. Insecure people don't make good mates or friends because they will end up being disloyal.

Become who it is you want to attract. In other words, if you want someone spiritual, become more spiritual. If you want an honest person in your life, become honest yourself, and look very closely at who you are.

What is honesty to you? What level of honesty are you willing to go to yourself? If you tell someone you will get back to them, do you respond and how long does it take? If you tell someone you'd like to take them to dinner, do you follow through or not? Check your honesty gauge first before expressing the intention that you want honest people in your life. Because you get exactly what you are putting out.

When I became honest with myself, I realized very quickly I had no idea of how to be intimate with another person. The word *intimacy* means "into me, see." Look into yourself, know yourself, and then you can begin to know another person.

journal page

Date: _____

The times I've been judged because of my appearance were:

This made me feel:

The times I judged another person based on appearance or what I've heard about that person have been:

chapter twenty-four

HOW TO **NOT** LEAD SOMEONE ON

There is a difference between how men and women feel about sex. A man can have sex and be perfectly fine never seeing that woman again. He can also orgasm every time he has sex regardless of whether he's in love with his partner or not.

A woman, on the other hand, is more emotional about sex. There are exceptions, but on average, the feminine woman is emotional about sex, and every sex act means something to a woman.

On the etheric level, every time a woman has intercourse with a man and he ejaculates inside her, she takes into her body and her spirit a part of the man's spirit. This is why it is vital to a woman whom she chooses to have sexual intercourse with, because along with a part of that man's spirit she absorbs some of his traits.

This is how a soul tie is formed. Once a man had ejaculated inside of his partner, a soul tie is crated between these two people and this sometimes takes lifetimes to undo. It isn't necessarily the same for men because they do not take in, so the burden falls more on the woman than on the man.

Women, choose wisely. If a female partner is taken by force or against their will, the male or males who have violated the other person sexually will be bound to each other in the realm of negativity. They will have multiple acts of violence committed against them, their children and their children's children. If the violent sex act results in death to the victim, they will have the same retribution and they, in turn, will die a violent death either in their present lifetime or in a future lifetime.

The victim must take a look at where she was consciously before the time of the attack. Through a cleansing meditation she must release the spirit of violence that was forced upon her and work on releasing the victim mentality so as not to attract any more violence.

Prayer and meditation and staying focused on being continually surrounded by light and by love will keep a person away from negative elements. If the person has passed into spirit because of this violent act, it is important for loved ones to pray that the spirit be protected, guided by love, and released with purity to God.

It is soulfully important to not lead another person on. If you meet someone you like or are attracted to but you know this person isn't "the one" let him/her know this up front.

If both partners agree up front that they are both aware and conscious that the relationship is temporary, then it's okay. If one person doesn't agree and wants to take it to another level, it is vital to break away from one another before a deep attachment on the physical level is formed and someone gets their heart wounded.

Again, refrain from leading another person on. To do so results in the build up of bad karma with this person and holds up your evolution. More importantly it keeps your true love from coning into your net.

journal page

Date: _____

List the times when you felt someone led you on.

_____ led me on. I felt these feelings when it happened.

I led on the following people:

I was aware or unaware of it at the time.

AFTERWORD

This book is a product of much trial and error. I've spent most of my life in the search of what it is that keeps a person in a negative state and how to get someone (myself included) into a positive state where attracting what we want is achievable.

I believe with every fiber of my being that your life can change on a dime, if you want it to. I also have the firm belief that when we know what it is that we want beyond a shadow of a doubt, we attract that very thing to us. It is unavoidable. When we focus on what we don't want, we become like a beacon and attract that into our lives as well.

When I became clear on what I wanted, one thing at a time, focused my energy on that one thing, and then released it into the universe, it manifested into my life.

I can remember there was a time when I was deeply depressed. I lost my beloved grandfather to suicide. Because of my grief and my lack of understanding of the grieving process, all I could think of was my pain. Instead of focusing on the big picture that the event had nothing to do with the years of joy, teachings, and love that I experienced because of my grandfather, I only focused on the mental picture of his death and that I perceived he was gone forever.

When I learned through NLP how to shrink the negative picture, put it in black and white, shove it out into the distance and dissolve it, then I began to climb out of the debilitating state I'd put myself into.

When I focused on all the fantastic times I shared with my grandfather, blew the picture up to where it was big and colorful in my mind, then I could get into a happy state whenever I wanted.

When I taught myself how to combine NLP with spirituality and learned about the different levels of consciousness, how death is merely a stepping into another form of energy, then I could heal.

During this process, I wrote a series of books for young adults. The first one called *Kelly Karate Encounters the Moon Princess*. It is about a young girl raised by her grandfather. When he dies unexpectedly, she becomes depressed and has an accident which results in her being in a deep coma.

While in the coma, Kelly goes into another dimension where she meets beings from another world. They are at war with an evil Dragon kingdom, and they ask for Kelly's help. Along the way, Kelly meets a wise old monk who guides her and teaches her that just because someone has physically died, it doesn't mean that the love they shared goes away. Kelly learns that love is eternal and once the power of that love is realized, the person will suddenly find themselves transformed from who they used to be into a more evolved person.

Like Kelly, I was in a coma, the coma of being unaware. Days and months went by where I just existed, feeling nothing, allowing abusive people into my life, abusing myself by drinking too much, feeling sorry for myself and giving my power away.

When I began to see that I wore a mask with many layers and started to peel the layers away one by one, I saw life in a different light.

Life is truly what <u>we</u> make of it. It can be a scary place filled with disappointments or it can be magical, blissful, and happy. Life can take us to heights you can create by entering the positive states of love, laughter, and joy. You can magnify those states a trillion times.

I am going to close this book with the words of one of the most beautiful souls I have ever met:

"Looking into your eyes in a mirror and seeing your magnificent soul smiling back at you, telling you without words — how amazing you are, how you make a difference by being alive, how your simple existence makes this world a better place — that is experiencing true love."
Laurie J. Driggers, Spiritual counselor

And remember that wherever you go, people fall in love with you. They don't know why, they just do.

Susan Barnes

Printed in the USA
CPSIA information can be obtained
at www.ICGtesting.com
JGIIW00221011 0021
68134JS00014B/536